THE BOLTONS
OF
THE LITTLE BOLTONS

By
Robert Philip Bolton

Also by Robert Philip Bolton
The Fable of Flitcroft Point
Jacko. One Bloke. One Year.
The Boys and Men of Auckland's Mickey Rooney Gang
The Fine Art of Kindness
Six Murders?
Underneath The Arclight
To The White Gate
My Marian Year
The Tapu Garden of Eden
The Collected Short Stories (in which is combined *Nana's Special Day
and other stories*, *The Dolphin and other stories*, and *Quickies.)*
For Viktor. The story of Mussorgsky's 'Pictures at an Exhibition'

Robert Philip Bolton was born in New Zealand in 1945. He has
been writing most of his adult life. Most of his work is about New
Zealand and New Zealanders. He lives in Auckland.

*Some of the source material used for this book
has been previously developed as short stories.*

For Kath

THE BOLTONS
OF
THE LITTLE BOLTONS

By
Robert Philip Bolton

Prologue

THIS IS A BOOK OF SMALL PORTRAITS OF SOME OF the many people my wife and I met in the course of a job we shared in a small corner of London for just a few months in nineteen ninety-two. There is no plot. There is nothing in it that is particularly dramatic or exciting. On the contrary it is concerned with the mundane; the daily routine of people who were interesting only because their way of life was strange, unsustainable and all but extinct. I could see that — surely any outsider could — but those concerned, the living subjects of my little portraits, clearly could not. To them everything in their world was perfectly normal. To me living there with them was like being in a dream based not in the present, nor even the past, but in some insubstantial, ethereal other-world that seemed to be fading away even as I lived in it.

Things in this curious other-world appeared perfectly normal. There were always plenty of normal people in busy streets lined with modern cars; red double-decker buses wove patiently through the thick traffic of the narrow Fulham Road and the King's Road, and black cabs rattled along the side streets taking clever shortcuts to Brompton Road and Cromwell Road. But to me, a visitor from distant and oh-so-different New Zealand, the busy streets felt empty and eerily haunted. Their tall, oversized black-brick houses, looking old, cold and damp, loomed and leaned over their mossy undersized gardens, evoking only the Victorian past. Ordinary, everyday events seemed to move with a purpose now obsolete and meaningless towards a non-existent objective. Some of the little shops looked quaintly old-fashioned and even some of the people in the streets seemed to belong more to another time, another era, like ghosts somewhat bewildered to find themselves disconnected from the place and out of joint with time.

The real names of the people I met are inconsequential and so have not been used; what's important is that they existed at all and that I chanced to glimpse their ghostly images just as they were fading away. It seemed I was present at — and part of — a sad and somewhat surreal and shabby end of an era, unmarked by history; a metaphor for the demise of what was once the greatest and richest city in the world, the capital of the world's most powerful empire.

Chapter I

FIRST, THE BELL. THE HARSH JANGLE OF A SERVANT-summonsing electric bell installed for emergencies above Kath's bed.

Then a shout.

'I say. Bolton! Bolton!'

It was the old man. His loud shout was full of fear, even panic.

Struggling out of the deep and dreamless sleep I so desperately needed — so long were our hours and so hard our work — and expecting the worst, I threw on my robe and went to our top floor landing. There, two landings below, was the old man in his white towelling robe now shading his eyes from the light I had just switched on.

'What is it? Is Mrs Beaumont all right?'

By now Kath was behind me.

'Mrs Bolton,' he said to Kath, ignoring me. 'I'm afraid the wife's had a bit of an accident.'

It was three o'clock in the morning.

It all started a year earlier when we — my wife Kath and I, then in our middle years — decided we needed a change. We had a successful little business in New Zealand that kept us busy and gave us financial security. We were surrounded by friends and families in one of the world's happiest, least populated and most unspoiled lands. We were happy, relaxed, contented, comfortable. And bored.

We'll do something 'different', we said. We'll change. At least for a while. We knew people of our age who had gone to Britain and worked managing castles and estates in remote parts of Yorkshire, Cornwall, Scotland, even the Isle of Wight and the Channel Islands. Some had done house-minding. Others had worked in pubs or on farms. We knew one man who had run a salmon-fishing farm in Scotland while his wife managed the property's little tea shop. So we'll go to Britain and find some interesting but undemanding work. The simple life.

'Physical work will be good for us,' I said.

'Not too physical,' said Kath.

'You know what I mean. Rest the brain for a change.'

Rest the brain. Get physically active and so give ourselves the chance to think; and to really look and listen to better understand what we see and hear.

'But where are you actually going?' we were asked. 'And what are you actually going to do?'

Questions to which we could reply only that we '—have no idea'.

But we did have some ideas. We had the right stamps in our passports. We planned to find live-in domestic work in Britain — anywhere in Britain — that would provide us with a home, a modest wage, a simple life, and the time and opportunity to explore another place and experience another way of life.

'Something completely different,' we said.

Internet and email use was not then universal, and was in fact rare in England, so we had begun by writing away for *The Lady* magazine, that odd and peculiarly English weekly publication which claims to have been 'in continuous publication since 1885' being 'widely respected as England's longest running weekly magazine for women'. It was an odd publication with a split personality: on the one hand its insubstantial articles — on life in town and country, dining, entertaining, overseas travel and the arts — appeared to be aimed at elderly women at, or aspiring to be at, the upper levels of 'society' while its many pages of tightly set classified advertisements — seeking au pairs, butlers, chauffeurs, companions, cooks, gardeners, housekeepers, lady's maids, mother's helps, nannies and more — were aimed directly at those standing on the bottom rung of the English social ladder seeking domestic positions 'at home and abroad'.

Obviously this flimsy little journal couldn't be sought and read by both markets; clearly its rather anaemic articles were there only to provide a genteel environment for the magazine's real purpose as a job market for servants.

We were interested in its advertisements for couples.

> SOUTH OF WINCHESTER. — Experienced couple, suit semi-retired persons. One to do light household duties in morning, other look after cars, swimming pool, help in garden, some DIY and driving. Mostly mornings, some afternoons, Two bedroom house provided. References essential.
>
> COUPLE NEEDED. — Caretaking small country house, Wiltshire. Part time duties, housekeeping, cooking, gardening, maintenance. Flexible arrangements considered. Own accommodation. References essential.
>
> COUPLE REQUIRED. — Experienced housekeeper/cook, gardener/handyperson for large house in Berkshire. Own two b/room house. Excellent conditions and salary.
>
> COUPLE REQUIRED. — Experienced cook/house-keeper and experienced gardener/handyperson required for busy family in Dorset manor house. Must like animals. Own cottage provided. References essential.

As well as these tiny advertisements there were display advertisements from agents, some specialising in placing couples, offering a variety of positions.

> OXON. Exp Butler/Chauff & HK/Cook for client with beautiful rural home. Drivers essen. Ideal cple will be drivers. 30s 40s with no pets or dependants. 2 bed house. 5 day wk.
>
> LONDON. HK/Cook & Houseperson/Driver to run international families lovely home. Beautiful 1 bed self-contained flat.
>
> GLOUCESTERSHIRE. Sought after position for top class Couple for large manor home catering for titled family + friends. Butlering, Driving, Managing, HK + Cook, etc (other staff). Own home, costs, etc.
>
> OXFORDSHIRE. Young and energetic Housekeeper/Cook and Butler/House Manager couple required for large country house. 2 bedroom cottage on estate. Generous package.

Evidently plenty of work for couples.

From home we wrote only to the agents seeking advice in advance but receiving only one reply. We weren't discouraged especially when we were told, by the many people whose example we were following, that the sort of work we were seeking was rarely arranged by post and that it would be easy once we were there in person to make our applications directly to the advertisers.

We had assembled a file of references to take with us but it wasn't easy. Our aptitude and adaptability — and a confidence in our ability to learn quickly and do anything — were not qualities easy to prove. Who would care to hire middle-aged, inexperienced domestic servants whose only credentials were based on their business experience at the other end of the world? So we sought references that referred, especially, to our personal qualities: our ability to work hard, to get on with people, to bring up children, to run a home. I knew, as all New Zealand men of my generation do, how to drive, repair machinery, work with wood and tools, maintain a house, run a garden and more; furthermore, and unlike most men of my generation, I was a confident cook and thoroughly enjoyed working in the kitchen. And as someone who had been an employer for many years I also knew what was expected of a good and loyal employee. For her part Kath had tried nursing as a student before qualifying as a school teacher; since then she had published children's books all over the world, managed a newspaper, been creative director in an advertising agency, and was a stepmother to that most difficult of species: teenaged boys.

Would it be enough? There was only one way to find out. And so, on a balmy summer's evening in February, nineteen-ninety-two, a year after making the decision to go, we said goodbye to our friends and family in the garden bar of the Northcote Tavern in Auckland.

And then, suddenly, from the bright light, warmth and clear summer skies of our southern hemisphere home in New Zealand we found ourselves in the grimy grey chill of a damp London winter. Our London-based niece was there to meet us and we bear-hugged each other through the unfamiliar thickness of our coats. The rest of our limited wardrobe was in the two backpacks and one small suitcase that lay on the cold wet concrete beside us outside the Heathrow terminal.

'Is this *all* your luggage?' Lisa asked. She had, foolishly perhaps, agreed to let us stay with her until we found a 'position'.

'That's it.'

We based ourselves in Lisa's flat in Wetherby Gardens and immediately began the work of looking for work. We started with the only letter we had received from a London domestic employment agency. Signed by the inevitable 'Miss', it sounded warm and encouraging, promising plenty of work and asking only that we made contact as soon as we arrived in London. And so that particular Miss was our first call but we discovered that she was missing and her little enterprise was no longer in business.

We bought the latest copy of *The Lady*, full of fresh new advertisements but sitting in the London gloom of Lisa's basement flat we found that there were now few opportunities for couples. To those few which sounded promising we hand-wrote formal letters of application but it was difficult and time-consuming to dash off to interviews all over England. And so, after a few fruitless days of wading through *The Lady*, and futile letter writing, we decided to start again by visiting only London agents — in person — and so get our names listed.

Our meetings with these agents marked our introduction to the people of this 'other' London and the beginning of our strange adventures.

I have no record of the number of agents we visited but they merge into one memory: a dingy, shabby office near but not quite within a fashionable West End, Knightsbridge or South Kensington neighbourhood. A sign, on or near the door, that was hard to find and, once found, was faded and hard to read. A narrow, crooked staircase rising to a couple of rooms of threadbare carpet, grubby paint, peeling wallpaper, and dust; flowers that were plastic and faded, calendars that were out of date, coffee instant, lights unshaded, desks ugly, chairs bursting their horsehair, and files — if that's what they were — lying randomly about the room.

The owner was almost always an overweight, badly dressed woman of late middle age. She was rarely pleasant to us but her tone and, intriguingly, her accent changed immediately when she made a phone call to, or received one from, a lady client. The clients, too, were always women; it seemed that the employment of servants was women's work.

Establishing a good agency name seemed important. Inherited Victorian or Edwardian beginnings were assumed whenever possible. Or humble origins, perhaps a little spinsterish or widowed hardship, were implied by the use of the founder's name with a title no grander than Miss or Mrs. The idea was to suggest that this was a small, simple business — rendered as a service to her betters, more from a sense of duty and respect than for money — founded by a retired plain-looking lady's maid of experience, refinement, impeccable credentials and an outmoded wardrobe; a woman so experienced that she, better than anyone else, would understand madam's needs and would, of course, have just the right contacts at the lower levels of society to find the perfect butler, valet, chauffeur, gardener, cook, maid, house parlour maid, nanny or companion.

Furthermore it all seemed based on a mutual delusion — mutual to the agency lady and her clients — that there actually existed a surplus of well-trained, honest and honourable men and women, preferably of the English race, whose only desire was to find a noble and benevolent employer to whom they could willingly dedicate the rest of their lives in decent and loyal servitude. The reality was that while such people did exist there was no surplus of them, and wise employers kept them happy, well paid and off the market. But, as I soon discovered, there were always the poor, the simple, the uneducated, the foreigners with little English — and even less understanding of English ways which are even more mysterious than the English language — who, together, constitute the largest resource of people prepared to do menial work for low wages in other people's houses.

The dynamics of these domestic employment agencies were quite simple and Miss Hart's *Staff Solutions Bureau* in Kensington was typical. To the side of the proprietor's desk was a narrow wooden box within which were arranged — presumably in some order — a line of white cards ruled in light blue and printed by hand or antique typewriter. At that time the New Zealand I had just left was highly computerised but not once in these dreary, depressing, grubby little offices did I see a computer or any suggestion of data-based logic or order. Whether Miss Hart's lidded box contained the records of employers or employees or both I couldn't decide but it was into it that she plunged a podgy, bejewelled hand. It was a random process and it seemed to me, as we waited, watched and listened, that it worked on the remarkable principle that at some fantastically lucky moment in the day the needs of a fabulously rich, generous, kind and desperate employer would happily and miraculously coincide with a poor, clever, experienced, desperate and very English employee meaning Miss Hart's benevolent little bureau would earn a commission.

I was astonished by this inefficient reliance on luck and coincidence. I felt that given but a couple of days I could have reorganised this tiny business, taught Miss Hart how to better care for her employer and employee resources, bought a cheap computer and a simple data-base programme, and started earning enough money to at least paint the walls, lay some carpet, and buy a decent coffee maker.

In the service of the little box of index cards, and in the absence of a computerised data base, there was an application questionnaire: a form that was badly laid out, with typed-in afterthoughts, twinks and deletions, all blurred and spotted by over-photocopying; a form that seemed to have been designed in Edwardian days, accurately reflecting the needs of Edwardian employers, turn-of-the-century employment conditions and the form-filling abilities of footmen, scullery maids and under-house parlour maids only briefly educated in rustic nineteenth century schools. We did our best, within the limited compass of this dreadful form, to suggest our talents and potential, submitting copies of references that may or may not have been ever read, and furnishing passport-size photographs.

Odd people came and went as we filled out the forms and waited. We spoke to one well-dressed and reasonably well-spoken elderly man. He appeared healthy and well, was tall and upright — he might once have been a guardsman — but looked close to seventy. And despite his proud bearing his eyes looked vacant and somewhat sad; I guessed he was disillusioned by a life that had not turned out quite as expected. No doubt it hurt and embarrassed him to have to visit these shabby offices and grovel to Miss Hart and other supercilious agency women like her.

'Barnes,' he said. 'Butler to Lord Corbury at Carstairs Manor.' The names meant nothing to me. 'Forty years man and boy.'

'What happened?'

'Died,' he said flatly. 'Found him meself. In the stables. On the floor. Covered in straw and muck he was.'

'Oh dear.'

What could I say?

'Nobody else,' he said. 'No family. No heirs.'

'So what about you?'

'Revenue got the money, National Trust got the house, hunt got the horses and hounds, club got the wine, and yours truly got the order of the boot.'

'Oh dear,' I said again.

'Need another gentleman now,' he said.

At that he lit up a cigarette — smoking inside was common and acceptable in England at that time — and never said another word.

Barnes was one of the few men we encountered. But there was a constant parade of women, of all ages and nationalities, willing to take anything Miss Hart had to offer. Generally large of body, and wrapped in cheap woollen coats, they gave these little places the steamy air of a war-time refugee camp; they struggled with language and form-filling, and tried — hopelessly I thought — to 'sell' themselves to the haughty proprietors. They looked miserable and depressed — altogether a miserable and depressing sight — and it was an altogether miserable and depressing experience to realise that we were in no more demand than they.

They were ripe for exploitation, and I felt sorry for them, but there was nothing I could do. It was probably just another day in the business life of the agency owners who must have been watching this parade of the hopeless for as long as they had been in business.

Back in the chill of Kensington High Street, knotting our scarves, pulling our woolly beanies down over our ears, drawing on our gloves, looking about for somewhere warm to have a cup of tea, it was obvious that despite all the advertisements in *The Lady* there was little if any demand for a couple like us; evidently we had managed to arrive at just the wrong time.

Suddenly we were sick of looking for work, sick of dealing with these silly agency women who lived lives of lies, deluding themselves and their poor exploited clients, and sick of the cold and the damp and the grime and the high cost of everything in London.

'It's not working is it?' I said.

'No, said Kath. 'It's not working. And neither are we.'

'No.'

And then we met Prudence.

Chapter II

PRUDENCE'S LITTLE BUSINESS WASN'T ESPECIALLY different from the others but she was younger than the other owners, more natural, less stuffy, nicer to us, and certainly better dressed. She seemed also to run a secretarial employment agency which meant she was more in touch with the nature and needs of people in the real world outside domestic service. Kath deduced, somehow, from something framed on the wall, that she had once placed a teenaged Lady Diana Spencer as an ironer of shirts for a young aristocrat in Colherne Court. It didn't make any difference to our prospects but Kath the Royalist was immensely impressed.

We liked Prudence at once and she liked us in return. And despite the fact that she also had a little wooden index box I did see a computer at work and felt encouraged enough to believe that, at last, we might be in the right place at the right time. And I was right; Prudence did have a client whose needs, by the sound of it, happily coincided with ours.

'But they don't really need a married couple,' she said.

Good start I thought.

'Actually I don't think they know what they need.'

Eh?

'It's awfully complicated.'

That didn't sound promising either.

She went on to explain that she had never met the actual clients; she was really working for the family, or at least for two daughters of the family.

'They're at their wit's end,' she said, somewhat mysteriously.

She went on to describe the situation as discreetly as she could, as she understood it from the daughters. Evidently the parents were old; in their late eighties, nearly ninety. The mother was infirm and needed help; not necessarily professional nursing help but assistance with bathing and dressing, and getting into and out of bed. She didn't get outdoors enough and needed to be taken for walks in her wheelchair. And, as much as anything, she needed a companion who could speak English, was pleasant, intelligent and mature.

'You speak English,' I said to Kath. 'One out of four.'

Prudence looked at Kath, then at me, and smiled indulgently. Patiently. Kath kicked me in the shins.

According to the family she — the lady client — was a dear, sweet old thing, no more crotchety and unreasonable than might be expected from someone of her age and infirmity.

But how infirm? We didn't ask. We listened; tried to look serious and interested.

Prudence then told us as much as she could about the old man which was very little. He was difficult — I wondered what 'difficult' meant — of that she was sure, but she was unable (or unwilling?) to provide details. Evidently he had driven other staff to tears and away with his rudeness. And that, she implied grimly, was part of the problem: she was simply running out of people she could place there.

'I thought you liked us,' I said. The patient Prudence merely smiled indulgently. Again. Kath kicked me in the shins. Again.

'I've just got nobody who will suit them,' she said.

They were rich and old — she was certain of that — and they lived, she told us with a smile, and a glance at our name on the application form, in The Little Boltons, one of the smartest and most expensive streets in Kensington.

'What a coincidence,' I said.

'It's an omen,' said Kath.

'It's so handy to everything,' said Prudence. 'You'd love it there. Really.'

Prudence had taken a liking to Kath. She could see that Kath was friendly and capable, and wiser than the young nurses who had previously occupied the position, and would therefore be perfect for the lady client.

'But what can we get *you* to do?' she asked me. 'I don't suppose you can cook.'

'I can cook,' I said brightly.

Evidently she didn't hear me. Or it didn't register.

'You see they need someone who can cook good old-fashioned English food.'

'That's right up my alley,' I said.

But again she seemed not to hear me.

'That's what they like. Plain old-fashioned English food They had a Filipino cook but…'

Poor Prudence's voice trailed off at that point implying, oh dear, that surely we must know all about Filipino cooks. So we nodded sagely. It was expected. But we knew nothing about Filipino or any other kind of cooks.

'I can do it,' I said. Insisted.

'Really? Cook?'

She sounded astonished. Was it really *that* unusual that a man should be a cook?

'Yes, really.'

She looked at Kath for confirmation.

'He can. Really,' said Kath.

'Old fashioned English food? Nothing fancy.'

'Yes. Exactly. Not fancy at all.'

Prudence looked thoroughly pleased. But cautious. Thoughtful. She put her elbows on the desk, clasped her hands together, rested her chin on them, and then, as if having made an important decision, looked directly and seriously at me. I leaned forward expectantly.

'That's brilliant,' she said. 'In more ways than one.'

I was puzzled by that. It must have shown.

'Well, you see, they, the daughters — there's another daughter, in the country, and a son too — they'd all love to have a man in the house but they never imagined — I mean, there's no need for a gardener, they have a lady come in every week, and no car to be driven, fixed or cleaned — a man cook. Imagine it.'

'I don't have to,' I said. 'I am one.'

'Yes,' she said, smiling again. She looked relieved. 'A comedian too, I see.'

'I can be very serious,' I said seriously. Prudence laughed.

'Yes. Well, you see, the old man — Mr Beaumont's his name — seems to hate foreigners and young girls so you can imagine how young foreign girls have done there. I've had my girls here in tears from his bullying.'

'Sounds awful,' said Kath.

'It was. But I don't think he'd do that to a man.

He'd better bloody not, I thought.

'Or to you,' she was looking at Kath, 'or anyone else, if there was a man in the house.

'He'd better not,' I said.

'No. Quite,' said Prudence.

So, despite being a little puzzled, Prudence followed her good instincts. She knew, probably from experience with the daughters, that Kath was ideal. Perhaps she hoped that if the daughters and the clients themselves liked Kath then surely they would accept the strange and unusual idea of a man cook.

And so the meeting ended. Prudence promised to talk to the daughters about us and our potential to solve their problem. She said that she'd get back to us within a week.

There was only one other opportunity: a wealthy American couple, with a flat in London, an estate in the country, homes all over America, and a beach house in the Florida Keys, wanted us to work for them. We were to spend half the year in their country house in England and the other half in their house in Florida. It sounded idyllic but they also wanted us to be less than honest when we entered the United States, saying we were there on vacation, to avoid immigration complications. From people who demanded absolute honesty from their staff it seemed an unusual request.

We declined that post and waited patiently for a meeting with Prudence's clients' daughters. We were getting desperate but we sensed from Prudence that they were too.

Chapter III

'THEY'RE NOT QUITE SURE,' PRUDENCE SAID ON THE phone, 'but I told them about you both, and when I showed them your references they decided they should at least meet you.'

We were to meet Hermione and Alice, the daughters of the lady client Mrs Beaumont, at Hermione's house. We received our instructions concerning streets, bus numbers and stops, and two evenings later found ourselves across the river near Putney bridge. It was dark and cold. Hermione's house was on a corner, the first, or last, of a long brick row.

We were still fascinated by the density of London's population, and the compact size of the houses and gardens. But although appearing small from the outside, in the dark, Hermione's house was roomy and the atmosphere warm and friendly.

Hermione was also warm and friendly, interesting and full of fun. Small and round, she bubbled over with energy and enthusiasm. I guessed that she was a little older than I, with a smooth skin free of creases but those at the eyes made by laughing, and a broad smile that was so cheerful it made me smile in return. As she spoke her hands were busy touching her fair hair or twisting a button at the neck of her dress. And her eyes widened occasionally, to emphasise a point, and I noticed that they really did sparkle. She was a delight.

She introduced her quiet sister, Alice, and we all moved into the living room. Alice was small, too, but slight. She appeared light, dainty and delicate, like a retired ballerina — perhaps now a ballet teacher — and her manner was gentle and more reserved than that of her sister. Her face, too, had an unlined look but was more tranquil, less animated; and its whiteness was framed by wavy black hair streaked with steel grey. Her eyes were penetrating and serious but not unkind, and when she spoke her voice was gentle and sweet.

We sat on a luxuriously soft couch near an electric fire, had coffee and nursed a fat cat, while Hermione and Alice took turns telling us about the 'position' and asking us more about ourselves. Of the position we learned much more than Prudence had been able to tell us but not — as we discovered later — all that was to be told. Their mother and her husband had each been widowed in their early sixties. They had met through a friend and had married in what they — their various children — still considered too much haste. Now, in their late eighties and approaching their twenty-fifth wedding anniversary, they had had plenty of time in which to repent, if necessary, at leisure. But apparently, despite their children's opinion, they were still perfectly happy.

They had lived in The Little Boltons these twenty-five years without incident even though Hermione and Alice worried that Mr Beaumont may not have been the husband their mother deserved. Now, while generally well, she was slightly incapacitated as a result of an fall — suffered, as I later learned, while holidaying in New Zealand — and so needed more help than she used to. But it seemed she carried on as normally as possible and was fiercely but not foolishly independent.

We listened and realised that underlying Hermione and Alice's explanations was the frustration that, because of their mother's desire for independence, and her husband's jealous resentment of outside interference, there was little they could do to help either of them in their declining years. Staff, they said, were a constant problem. Now, with the departure — they looked at each other and rolled their eyes as they said 'departure' — of the Filipino cook, (we nodded knowingly but in fact knew nothing of the Filipino cook nor of her 'departure'), there was the opportunity to 'plant' someone of their own choosing in the house; someone who could and would do more, with more intelligence and more care, than just another servant hired from just another agency; someone who could and would watch and listen while working, and accurately report to them on Mr and Mrs Beaumont's health and welfare.

According to Hermione and Alice Mr Beaumont's only family, a daughter called Celia, had her own concerns about her father: his failing memory, his increasing irritability, the way he was becoming careless about his appearance, and, more than anything, the way he kept her at a distance. Apparently he had always been a difficult father but nevertheless her concern for his welfare was steadfast.

Clearly we were being asked to engage in a conspiracy. It seemed that because we were mature, intelligent and English-speaking we might provide the means — a rare chance — by which family members could discover what went on within a home where staff spent more time with their parents than they ever could; a chance to discover how well, or unwell, the old pair were, and how they really coped with daily life; a chance granted by Mrs Beaumont only because now, so late in life, the idea of interviewing staff and making decisions was too tiresome. She had agreed that if Hermione and Alice could find someone suitable she would conduct her own interview to satisfy herself about their choice. And, because hiring staff was women's work, Mr Beaumont would naturally agree with her decision. And that would be that.

But where to find such a person or persons willing to join in this conspiracy? Could we do it? Would we do it? We assured them that we had no doubt we *could* do it. And *would* do it. Absolutely. Except it seemed very vague. What exactly *were* we to do?

So we listened. Hermione and Alice's idea of what had to be done was naturally coloured by their desire to look after their mother's welfare. But they were also aware, and made it plain, that Mr Beaumont had needs too but they, and even his own daughter Celia, were uncertain of quite what they were

The basic idea seemed to be to 'keep an eye on him'; hardly a satisfactory job description when the conspiracy required that we did our eye-keeping while appearing to do useful and necessary work within the house. If we — or more especially I — were to keep an eye on Mr Beaumont without his realising it, we — and especially I — would have to have some meaningful work.

Hermione and Alice obviously trusted Kath. Clinically qualified nurses had been 'too professional' and had lacked the simple kindness, understanding, empathy and flexibility Mrs Beaumont needed. They could see that Kath, with her experience, common sense and maturity, would be fine for Mrs Beaumont. But could I *really* run the kitchen and do the cooking and shopping?

'Of course I could,' I said.

'Of course he could,' said Kath.

'Could you?' they asked, surprised. 'Good old-fashioned English cooking?'

'The only kind I know,' I said, which was true.

They looked at each other somewhat doubtfully.

'It sounds to me that taking care of your mother is a full time job,' I said.

'Oh, it is,' they said together, with a groan, obviously recalling personal experience. They and Celia had been sharing the responsibilities of looking after the old pair since the departure of the mysterious Filipino cook.

'Well then,' I went on, 'Kath can take care of your mother and I'll cook and run the kitchen.'

'Splendid,' said Hermione. 'But first you must meet mummy.'

Chapter IV

TWO DAYS LATER, A SATURDAY, WE MADE OUR WAY TO meet 'mummy' at The Little Boltons. We caught one of those old-fashioned London double-decker buses, the Routemaster model, which even then was being phased out. Short, squat and shabby, and painted a darker red than its newer cousins, it had a sealed half-cabin for the driver and a wooden platform at the back upon which the conductor swayed on spread legs. He nodded to us inside, sitting anxiously in our sideways seat, when we reached our stop on the Fulham Road.

The air was icy cold and a nasty wind stung our ears and nipped at our toes through our lightweight sneakers. We pressed woollen-gloved hands more deeply into our New Zealand sheepskin coat pockets and walked briskly up Hollywood Road. There were a few small restaurants there but the street mostly comprised little joined-up terrace houses that at home would be considered merely adequate as somewhere to live. But these, we knew, were desirable and expensive; the sort of little Kensington and Chelsea town houses from which we had seen emerging — on television at least — famous people, the Princess of Wales perhaps, closing a brightly-coloured door and dashing, head down, to a waiting car. Film stars, we were told, lived there, as did various members of western- and eastern Europe's obscure and forgotten royal families.

A car stopped, a dark BMW, and a well-spoken, well-dressed young man leaned out the window and tried to sell us an expensive-looking watch.

'Salesman's samples,' he said. 'Don't need them anymore.'

Did we really look that naive? We declined, politely, and moved on. A pub, The Hollywood Arms, looked closed and unwelcoming. A small wine shop which was later part of a rather unpleasant experience I had with Mr Beaumont. A little corner shop, with trays of limp vegetables and stale fruit set outside, lit up the wintry gloom with a yellowness reflected on the wet street. In Tregunter Road the houses were suddenly bigger, taller, grander. White-painted or plain brick, with heavy, varnished doors and large blank windows, they presented a stern face to the passer-by. Both sides of these streets, like most streets in the area, were lined with parked cars there being no room for car garages on these small plots of land whose houses were built before Henry Ford was even born.

And then, suddenly, we saw it: a large, white, reflective sign attached to the corner wall and embossed in black and red. 'The Royal Borough of Kensington and Chelsea', it said in Gothic type, and, below but larger, 'The Little Boltons SW10'. Knowing that the time was right we turned into the street with our name and made our way to the number we were seeking.

We stopped for a moment at the tall gatepost which was surmounted by an ornate lamp. The house was large — three stories above ground, one below — but it wasn't a mansion. It was a strange sight to us. Our house at home was not as tall but was otherwise as large if not larger than this, standing on its own, on land more open and broad, with a sweeping driveway to a double garage, and friendly neighbours at a distance of more than the entire width of this little parcel of London land. But this house was attached to its neighbour on the right while a neighbouring house rose hard on its left. Altogether it looked cramped for space and a little shabby and stooped; the white paint was flaking from the concrete and the door varnish was dulled. I notice that the garden seemed but half-cared for, that dead leaves had collected in the corners and on the steps, and that the path tiles were cracked and broken.

There was a short narrow path on the left boundary at the end of which I could see a cramped, dark, wet, descending staircase of mossy bricks. It was down there — where the drains entered the buried pipes, a place which Londoners call 'the area' — and up again that I was destined to go often in my duties.

But on this day it was at the front door we had to stand. We climbed the broad stairs to the varnished door with its dull brass furniture. The knocker or the bell? We chose the bell. We heard it ring inside. We heard murmuring; soft footfalls. We stood in the cold, removing our gloves, loosening our scarves, and arranging our papers in the plastic shopping bag that Kath carried at her side.

I wondered who would come to the door, Hermione or Alice. At last the heavy door opened. We were touched by a waft of warm air. A strange woman was there. Middle-aged. Smiling. A hushed greeting. A warm handshake across the threshold. Silence and darkness beyond.

'Hello, I'm Celia. Do come in out of the cold.'

We entered the entrance hall and stood while Celia took our coats and scarves, introduced herself as Mr Beaumont's daughter, and took the time, without embarrassment, to look us up and down. She was small and thin and seemed to do everything with tiny, nervous movements. But she had a kind, pleasant face, a nice smile and a quiet voice.

We had been told that she lived somewhere in the country but that she made frequent trips to London and normally took every opportunity she had to visit The Little Boltons. But with the departure of the mysterious Filipino cook it had been necessary for her to establish herself in the house, in a servant-like role, until new staff could be employed. Perhaps for that reason she looked worn, as if under stress, and seemed glad to meet us, perhaps relieved that we were neither young nor Filipino.

Standing in the hall talking I had time to notice only that the furniture — a large table and an elaborate coat-stand — was dark and old, and that the staircase disappearing upwards in front of us was fitted with a electric-powered elevator chair. The chair's seat was up, like a cinema chair, and a control arm was raised beside it as if in salute. I also sensed that the parquet flooring was over-polished — I learned later that dear Mariana, the daily housekeeper, took a lot of pride in that polished floor — making the soft old rug, that lay loosely in the centre of the hall, slippery and dangerous, and I wondered how a disabled old lady could manage it.

'In here,' said Celia.

She opened a door to the right of the staircase and we entered the living room. It was a large, bright room, carpeted in a faded *eau de nil* that went the entire depth of the house, from front to back. The back, looking out through the French doors and into the garden, was taken up by the dining suite and various cabinets. And I noticed an odd square, like a trapdoor, set into the carpeted floor close to the wall; somehow I knew that square of carpet was important, and so it turned out to be.

A large bookcase with glass doors was built into the wall marking the notional division between the dining and lounge areas. At the front of the room were two large windows, with full length green drapes and concealed shutters, which looked out onto the street. Below these a large, pale green and soft-looking couch and matching armchairs were loosely arranged around a low table; a small television set on a wheeled base looked high-tech and out of place.

Mr Beaumont was seated in one of the low chairs, and the coffee table in front of him was littered with newspapers. The comfortable chairs were evidently too low for Mrs Beaumont as she was sitting in her own firm, straight-backed armchair. A Zimmer — the English name for a light, four-legged walking frame with rubber hand-grips — stood within reach.

Mrs Beaumont looked like an older Hermione. Small and round, with a round face, she had a clear complexion, strong blue eyes, generous lips, and pure white hair brushed back naturally in a short unfussy style. As we came in she tried to stand but then, as if only then remembering how difficult and unnecessary it was, she relaxed back into her chair and extended her hand, limp and palm downwards. Her smile was broad, sincere and a little shy, but she looked up at each of us directly as we shook hands and then waited, not altogether patiently, as we were introduced to her husband. I noticed at once that she was slightly deaf and this, and her reduced mobility, obviously irritated her.

Mr Beaumont raised himself from the depth and comfort of his armchair to make his handshakes. He had a large hand and it grasped mine in a firm grip as, for the first time since my school days, I found myself addressed by only my surname although he pronounced it 'beau', as he would his own, rather than the 'bowl' which was the usual New Zealand pronunciation of Bolton. He called Kath Mrs Bolton and then seemed to dismiss her as not worthy of his interest. But he was intrigued by me, perhaps only because I was a man, and I was certainly intrigued by him. Once we had shaken hands he slouched back into his chair, throwing his right arm over its back in a casual pose, crossed his legs and peered over his bifocals at me with a look between condescension and impolite amusement, all obviously contrived for effect.

Tea and cakes appeared — I didn't notice how nor from where — and the talk was small. Mrs Beaumont seemed genuinely interested in us, where we came from, why we were now in England, how we liked London, how we liked the street and the house. Unlike most even slightly deaf people she spoke with a soft voice and I noticed that she always smiled slightly as she spoke, her head to one side, as if waiting to be amused, ready to laugh, wanting to discover something entertaining or amusing. She had a natural shyness that was perfectly charming.

Aware of both her deafness and our accents we tried to speak slowly and carefully; still she strained forward, always smiling, the better to catch whatever we might say. Yet sometimes, I could tell from her puzzled look, she couldn't really understand the way we said our words or framed our sentences. But she nodded and smiled anyway, closing her eyes briefly, either too polite or too tired to pursue the subject.

'You must see the kitchen?' she said.

'Oh, yes,' I said, uncertain of how I was expected to respond.

'It's lovely,' she said seriously. 'I used to spend a lot of time there. Harold and I used to entertain an awful lot you know.'

Harold? I guessed Mr Beaumont was Harold.

'We used to have such a lovely time you know. We knew everyone in the street. Such a lovely street. And such a pleasant part of London don't you think?'

'I like it here very much,' I said. And I did.

'Do you like to cook?'

'Oh, yes.' And I meant that, too.

'Harold and I like plain English food you know.'

'I understand,' I said, reassuringly I hoped.

'How did you learn? You're not a chef?'

'No,' I smiled. 'I'm not a chef. I learned by doing it. I enjoy it. Cooking for my family.'

'You have children?' She was genuinely interested. 'How many? Where are they now?'

Obviously she hadn't read our carefully-prepared notes. I didn't feel like telling her my life story. It was complicated, and she was deaf, so I evaded the question as best I could.

'There are three of them,' I replied. 'One in Australia, two in New Zealand. Living their own lives now. They don't need us anymore.'

'No. I see.' She smiled, as if understanding, and then turned to Kath.

And that was it. I was expecting more. Perhaps some hard-nosed negotiation. But Mrs Beaumont seemed perfectly satisfied, at least with me, and was now concentrating on Kath.

Chapter V

THE WOMEN'S CONVERSATION WAS OF NO INTEREST to Mr Beaumont so when it appeared Mrs Beaumont had finished with me, even before I had finished my tea, he stood up and steered me cleverly to the other end of the room where we stood together at the French doors looking out into the back garden.

'The garden,' he said.

'Nice,' I said, nodding.

It looked bleak and thoroughly un-nice to me but I could see, through the gloom, that it would probably be pleasant and attractive on a warm sunny day. It was divided in half down its length by a wide, straight path and was surrounded by a high, mossy walls overhung with leafless trees. Their winter branches looked like thin, black ink lines scratched on grey cardboard.

'Bought the freehold after the war,' he said. 'Good show. Best thing I ever did.'

He was a large but not especially tall man; the sort that was big in presence, like an overbearing village policeman, a comparison I realised he would not appreciate. He had a large head, not entirely bald, with wisps of white hair growing long over his collar, and he habitually ran his open hand over it from brow to neck. He was smartly dressed in a blue three-piece suit, properly buttoned, with what I thought was a gold watch-chain across his portliness, a tie set just-so, and black shoes.

'Second wife,' he said, not quietly. I glanced quickly to the front of the room but the women were still talking. 'First one died you know.' His eyes darted to the ceiling. 'Upstairs.'

He looked down at his shoes suddenly. I thought there was something on the floor but there was nothing. He shook his lowered head slowly. Then raised it slowly and heavily, like a old rhinoceros, and turned it towards the garden again.

He was standing beside me, legs apart, slightly hunched. One hand was in his trouser pocket and the other gripped the lapel of his coat in the manner of a stage barrister. It was a pose, carefully rehearsed, which went, I realised, with the small talk. Accordingly, I knew it would take its course and soon run out. And then what?

'Australia was it?'

'No. New Zealand.'

'Ah. New Zealand. Been there. Twice I think. With the wife. Canberra.'

'That's Australia.'

'No. Bally ship. Liner. Canberra. Round the world. Auckland. Spent some time there, you know.'

'Did you?'

'Dashed nuisance. Wife, this one, did her hip in on the ship. Hasn't been the same since. Hospital. Good place. Bones.'

'Ah,' I said, getting the drift. 'Middlemore hospital. It's an orthopaedic hospital.'

'Don't know. Ask the wife. She'll remember. It's going you know. Bally nuisance.'

'Is it?' I asked.

'Oh, yes. Can't remember a damned thing.'

He pushed his large head forward, towards me, and raised his eyebrows as if surprised.

'I was bright boy at school though, you know. Jolly bright little chap. In the cabinet. Prizes.'

'Really?' I couldn't have cared less.

'Oh, yes. Books. Never read them. Engraved. Show you some time. Ministry of Food.'

'Oh?' I said.

'The war, you know. Wales. Under—' and he mentioned a hyphenated name which meant nothing to me.

'Bally fool he was,' he said emphatically. He stood there beside me, hunched over again, shaking his head slowly with assumed disgust. 'Complete ass.'

Close to him now I could understand the family's concern. His shirt was frayed at the collar and sleeves, and his tie and waistcoat were spotted with food and grease. I even noticed that his shoes needed a polish. He obviously had a mental image of himself looking dapper, like the 'City Gent' he once was, but the smartness of his dress was an illusion that did not stand close inspection. Across the room I could hear the women — Mrs Beaumont, Celia and Kath — talking about the work, the conditions, the wages, the time off, when we might start. These were subjects of vital interest to me. I wanted to be part of the discussion.

Suddenly the old man raised his head and said: 'Don't sound it.'

He was staring at me intently.

'What?'

'Australian. I can understand you. Pretty decent.'

Pretty damn decent of you to say so, I thought.

'I'm from New Zealand,' I said. 'Perhaps we have a more English accent.'

He set his jaw and glared at me again over his glasses.

'Still colonials though.'

Colonials?

'Don't mind New Zealanders. It's a good street.'

'It has our name.' I was getting used to this way of talking.

'What's that?'

'Our name. Bolton.'

'Knew a Bolton once. Cliff Bolton. At school. Naughty chap as I recall. Always in trouble.' He chuckled to himself and then, apparently concerned, added suddenly: 'You're not related to him are you?'

He was staring at me again. Accusingly.

'I doubt it.'

He didn't seem interested in what was happening at the other end of the room, nor that I might soon be his employee. I'm not even sure if he knew who we were and why we were there. And then I was rescued by a call from Kath and I returned to the conference. Mr Beaumont followed me and returned to his place on the couch.

'Mrs Beaumont and I have agreed—' said Kath, speaking slowly and carefully, restating the proposed terms of employment, more for Mrs Beaumont and Celia's benefit than mine, and watching as Mrs Beaumont, straining forward to hear, nodded her agreement at each point. Celia was also nodding, and smiling broadly, probably with relief that she would soon be able to return to her own home.

'But what about—' I began but stopped when I received the wifely signal all men recognise as meaning: shut up; we'll talk about it later.

Mr Beaumont's participation was limited to dealing with the wages, the records, the taxes. He had been a career accountant but his contribution to the present discussion seemed rehearsed — rather like our discussion at the French doors — and he was not really interested in the financial or any other details at all. He seemed more interested in making an impression about his financial skills and his long-standing relationship with what he called 'the revenue'. He was leafing through our papers, glancing briefly at each, one of which was a character reference from our accountant, the partner of a large international firm. He recognised the stationery.

'Know this firm,' he said, waving the letter. 'Different name then.'

'They're a big firm all over the world,' I said.

He looked at me over his glasses, puzzled, slowly moving his jaw from side to side, wondering how a colonial manservant should know about large chartered accounting firms.

'I was in The City, you know,' he continued suddenly. 'Chartered accountant. Partner. Big firm. Bigger than this.'

I nodded to show that I was interested which I was not.

'Barton Mayhew, Alderman's House, Bishopgate, EC2,' he said. 'Director of internal audit and accounting procedure. That's why I run a tight ship here. Tight ship.'

Aye, aye, sir.

I was longing to formalise the terms and conditions referred to so vaguely by Kath. And I remembered the advice we had received from Prudence. 'You must get a contract,' she had said. 'You must have everything — your duties, your wages, your arrangements for time off, everything — in writing. Otherwise, believe me, you'll get taken advantage of. It happens all the time.'

So this was my chance. I raised the subject.

The old man's face immediately clouded over and he set his jaw in a way that I was becoming used to.

'Never had a contract. Never heard of such a thing.'

In The City. Chartered accountant. Partner. Big firm. Never had a contract. Never heard of such a thing.

I dropped the subject at once. We'd have to sort this out later.

So, were we employed? Did we have the job? I still didn't know.

Chapter VI

'NOW,' SAID CELIA, STANDING UP AND CLASPING HER hands in front in an impatient 'well, that's that' attitude. 'I'll show you around the house. Is that all right, Milly?'

Mr Beaumont's family called her by a diminutive of her first name, Millicent.

'Oh, yes, dear,' said Mrs Beaumont. 'Splendid.'

So we followed Celia out of the room, she turned and shut the door, and we were back in the dark hallway.

'I'll show you the room first,' she said going up the stairs ahead of us past the parked electric chair.

The room? What room? I looked at Kath — puzzled — but she just smiled and shrugged. We reached the top of the stairs, turned and climbed another flight.

'This was the family home, you know,' Celia said over her shoulder when we were out of hearing of the people below. 'Father's lived here continuously since he and my mother got married. He leased it at first, of course, but managed to buy the freehold after the war.'

She stopped and looked down at me frankly.

'He told you that didn't he.'

It wasn't a question and she sounded hurt and resigned.

'Yes. He told me that.'

'He repeats himself a lot,' she said.

Really? I hadn't noticed.

More closed doors.

'The guest-room,' said Celia indicating the door on the left. 'This is where I've been sleeping. Mariana stays here sometimes. She's the daily. Various nurses have slept here too. It used to be my room as a child.'

She opened another door.

'The main bedroom,' she said. 'My mother was always ill you know. She died here. He told you that, too, didn't he.'

We were allowed only a quick peep into the room and saw nothing but more large windows which I knew must look over The Little Boltons.

'Yes,' I said, solemnly, mildly embarrassed.

But it wasn't my fault. He just told me.

She looked at me for a moment, thinking. Thinking what? Then, indicating casually to this door and that, said: 'That's Milly's bathroom and that's father's study.'

At the next landing, another closed door.

'Father's bathroom.'

More stairs ahead of us but Celia stopped.

'Father's a very odd and difficult man you know,' she said, seriously. 'But perhaps it would be different—' she was looking at me again, '—with you.'

Me?

'Would it?'

'Yes. I think so. He doesn't dare bully men, you see,' she said. 'Milly needs help but father's been so intolerant of the people we've had before. He just drives them away. He can't help himself. It's an awful worry.

'He needs help himself,' she continued. 'But he won't accept any help or advice from anyone. Including us. The only person he tolerates is Mariana. She can say anything to him and he just laughs. You'll meet Mariana. She's been here for, oh, I don't know, absolutely ages.'

And then: 'You must make him get a haircut.'

A haircut. I made a mental note.

'You see, I don't want him to turn into a grubby, dribbling old man.'

Well, I thought, neither do I.

'And see if you can make him change his shirt. He has dozens of new shirts in his drawers. Never opened.'

Change shirts.

'What about Mrs Beaumont?' asked Kath.

Celia stopped. We were on another landing.

'It's funny, you know,' she Celia, turning to Kath, and resting her open right hand in her open left hand in front of her. 'She needs so much help. But she won't let me do it and I'd be so willing.'

I sensed that Celia cared for her father's wife more than she could say.

'It's not just me,' she said. 'She won't let Hermione or Alice help either; her own daughters. A generation thing I suppose. But she lets the nurses do anything.'

She sounded a little resentful. Or disappointed. Sad, maybe. Or hurt.

We climbed another staircase — the only one without an electric chair — and so to the top floor, our floor. At last. Here there was another bathroom lined with the white tiles and heavy porcelain equipment of the nineteen-forties. And two bedrooms. If the job were ours — and I still didn't know if it was — the bathroom and larger bedroom would be ours.

I went into the bedroom. The carpet was worn, the furniture was old and the paint was tired, faded, stained and flaking. The twin beds, with horsehair mattresses and feather pillows, had been freshly made and covered with fringed candlewick spreads; unmatched reading lights had been placed on the side tables, and the two pieces of large antique furniture — a walnut chest of drawers and a dark wardrobe — were thirsty for polish.

There was only one window, much smaller than those on the other floors, but it looked down over the back garden — the same garden I had been looking at from the ground floor — from a great height providing a long view across the neighbouring gardens, through a forest of leafless trees, to the sharp needle steeple of Saint Mary The Boltons. I paused there: it was a beautiful and tranquil scene. Beside the window stood a porcelain sink, with old brass taps and exposed plumbing below. But the room was spacious and yet had an intimate and friendly atmosphere, quite different from the other rooms in the house; I felt comfortable in it at once.

But Celia began to apologise.

'This floor hasn't been renovated for such a long time,' she said. 'Father never comes up here — he can't without the chair — so he doesn't really know its condition.'

He never comes up here.

'It's just fine,' I said. 'We'll be very comfortable here.'

I said it. And I meant it. Thanks to the absence of the electric chair we would have the privacy of our own floor. Two bedrooms including ours overlooking the garden, and a bathroom overlooking The Little Boltons. We would have somewhere to live, a goodly wage (I hoped), and the prospect of an interesting experience with interesting people. In London.

It seemed better that we had hoped when we started dreaming and planning a full year earlier. Sitting on our deck at home. Watching the southern hemisphere sun go down on another summer's day.

The summer sun will be coming up at home right now, I thought as I looked out into the chilly London garden and felt the warmth rising from an ancient skeletal radiator fixed below the window.

We left the room and trailed off downstairs again, past the electric chairs, to the ground floor. Opposite the front door was Mrs Beaumont's study — I hadn't noticed that room before — and a narrow hall leading to the back of the house and a door which opened onto a concrete landing and thence down to the garden. But there was yet another landing, and another staircase — this one enclosed in frosted glass, with its own glazed door — going down to the servants' hall below ground. These stairs were steel-edged and uncarpeted and we followed Celia down them noisily past yet another electric chair.

'It's very old-fashioned I know,' Celia was saying, 'but they have a routine and they like to stick to it. They both get very upset if things go wrong.'

They get upset if things go wrong.

We were standing in the kitchen. In nineteen-fifty it would have been a model kitchen worthy of a photo-spread in a decorating magazine. Its once fashionable cream and pale blue — almost everything below stairs was the same cream — were now faded, stained with smoke and dirty with grease. A caterer's gas cooker stood against one wall while a long stainless-steel bench with double sinks, a broken waste-disposer and a rusty dishwasher were lined up opposite. There were cupboards everywhere. A small refrigerator and freezer, bright and white and sharp-cornered, stood under a counter. Two high racks above the sink were loaded with restaurant-sized pots and pans. There was a large casement window at the end of the room — the only unbarred window on the floor — which opened into a small sunken area of cracked and broken concrete, littered with paper scraps and small stones — in the centre of which stood an ailing bay tree. An old but newly-white-painted table stood in front of the window.

In the corner of the room rested a monstrous dumb waiter with its motor, wheels, cables, gears, chains and counterweights on open display. Obviously it went up to the room above and explained the trapdoor I had noticed earlier.

'They rise at seven,' Celia was saying, 'and you'll have to help Mrs Beaumont. Then they come down to breakfast which has to be served at eight-thirty. That's followed by coffee in the lounge. There's a light luncheon at one, tea at four and supper at seven-thirty.'

What? All they do is eat. And they call the evening meal 'supper'. How will I remember all this? And they get upset if things go wrong.

'And, oh,' she added. 'Milly can't stand waste. You mustn't waste the food.'

Mustn't waste the food.

On we went, behind Celia, trying to take it all in. A large servants' living room was comfortably furnished and theoretically would be ours in the evening although, as it turned out, it never was. There was a concrete-floored laundry, a walk-in pantry, a cavernous but redundant coal cellar, a cooling room, various steel cabinets stacked with expensive but dusty china and crystal, and a tall, lockable steel cupboard full of wine, spirits and mixers.

'Don't *ever* go in there,' Celia said darkly. 'Father's always been obsessed with the idea that servants steal his wine.'

Don't steal his wine.

I noticed a door which opened to the side of the house below ground level; it was the entrance for servants and tradesmen which Londoners refer to as 'the area'. Another door opened to a garden courtyard and the downstairs toilet that was there for servants. Outside.

And that was it.

We weren't invited to return to the living room to farewell our potential employers but stood with Celia in the front hall collecting our coats and preparing to leave.

'There's so much more to tell you,' said Celia nervously as we stood together.

'Don't worry,' Kath said reassuringly. 'We'll learn our own way. They'll be all right. We'll look after them. And we can start as soon as you like.'

Celia's expression changed at once. She looked shocked.

'Oh, we'll see about that later,' she said, rather coolly. 'I have to get back home — I have my own family to look after, too — but I'll be talking to Hermione and Alice tonight and no doubt they'll be talking to Milly and someone will get back to the agent soon.'

Outside in the cold Kath said she felt deflated by Celia's parting words.

'I thought we had it for sure,' she said.

'We haven't got a contract or anything,' I said.

'We haven't got a job yet. Let's wait and see what happens next.'

We waited. But what happened next was nothing. We phoned Prudence and she promised to phone back but didn't. Accustomed to action, and used to making decisions for ourselves, we were frustrated by English slowness and inefficiency.

We discovered later that the family had taken the time to verify our references, waiting for the middle of the English night to phone during the New Zealand day to check that the chief accountants and mayors who had commended us so highly were real people who meant what they had said. Not knowing that at the time, but confident that the job would eventually be ours, and anxious not to outstay our welcome with our niece Lisa, we took a trip to the west of England, phoning Prudence whenever we could. Finally, one freezing Wednesday in February, standing at an open phone booth in Bristol, we received the news we wanted.

We had the job. When could we start? They needed us urgently.

'But we still haven't got a contract,' I whispered to Kath who was on the phone. She ignored me.

'We'll start on Monday,' she said into the phone. 'We'll move in our things on Sunday afternoon and we'll start on Monday morning.'

She hung up.

'What's happening?'

'She said Celia will be there on Sunday afternoon to show us the ropes,' said Kath, pulling on her gloves. 'But she'll be leaving after that.'

'And?'

'Well, come Monday morning we'll be on our own.'

'But we still don't have a contract. Prudence said—'

'She didn't mention it just now. I don't think we'll ever have a contract. Honestly. Do you?'

Chapter VII

AFTER SIX WEEKS OF RUNNING THE HOUSE ALONE Celia was anxious to get home to her own family. Thus she left the house that Sunday night, train ticket in hand, just as soon as she reasonably could after we arrived. The promised briefing was therefore brief.

Although we were not meant to start until the next morning, Monday morning, Kath's help was required almost immediately that Sunday night. It was the first but not the last time we observed the odd relationship between employer and servant when they live in the same house. Unlike the detached, remote association between most employers and employees, living together under the same roof — the employer's roof — inevitably puts servants at a disadvantage and makes their relationship with the employer peculiarly close and personal. This was even more so in the case of the disabled Mrs Beaumont who truly needed her servant's help just to get around.

Perhaps in the past, with generations of class conditioning and training, English servants had no emotional connection to their employer; perhaps experience had taught that it was impossible and unwise for servants to care about their employers. And history shows that English upper-class employers were generally kind and considerate to their servants in much the same way, and for the same reasons, that they cared for their horses and hounds: they needed them.

It was an odd arrangement that must have worked in the past but in nineteen-ninety-two, fresh from the 'colonies', without the conditioning of a English upbringing, and with no respect for England's absurd class-based attitudes, we found it impossible to consider ourselves 'servants' or 'servile' or anything but the equal of our employers. They were old people with a problem. They could have been our parents, our grandparents or our neighbours. On this occasion they were our employers, we were their employees. It was a job. But that did not mean we were inferior or servile. Nor did it mean we were or could be heartless.

And so, at the end of that first Sunday — once Celia had left but before our official Monday morning start — Kath had to help Mrs Beaumont to bed. We may not have been officially employed but she had no choice: the disabled old lady simply couldn't manage on her own. And so we discovered how easy it is for employers to exploit their servants even if only unconsciously. In this case the servant (Kath), not even officially employed, had to do something for the employer (Mrs Beaumont) — getting her undressed and into bed — that she could not possibly do for herself. The heartless withholding of that service by Kath — even if justified — was impossible. Guilt? Duty? Obligation? Kindness? Pity? Compassion? Whatever it was it amounted to a mild if thoughtless exploitation.

It was hard to demonise an employer who was merely an old and disabled lady — with whom we had to live — who needed help just to get into bed. But it was an ominous beginning.

The next morning, and every morning thereafter, we were up at seven. And each day began the same.

I was already awake when I heard the alarm clock from Mr Beaumont's room below. Then a series of bumps and noises signalled that he was getting up; donning dressing gown and slippers was noisy work.

I lay there for a while, listening, having slept better than ever in my adult life. I knew that tiredness of the brain, stress, keeps us awake — I was used to insomnia — but that tiredness of the body puts us to sleep. Because we worked almost constantly, from seven in the morning until nine or ten every night, I went to bed not merely tired but physically exhausted; consequently I slept like an infant. It was wonderful to sleep so well and wake up entirely refreshed.

The old bed was firm but cosy and the room was warm. I heard Mr Beaumont making his way out of his room to the electric chair.

There was the metallic sound of the chair's seat and arm going down, and then the whining of the electric motor as he was carried down to the next level. I soon recognised each sound and knew exactly what he was doing and what would happen next.

Seat and arm were then raised on chair one and lowered on chair two and the whining sound reached me again as he glided down to the ground floor. During his journeys he sat passively staring blankly ahead, his hand on the controls, waiting for the chair to stop. Then came more crashing noises as seat and arm were again raised out of the way. Then he padded across the hall to unlock and unbolt the front door — five actions were required before the door was completely free —and collect the newspapers from the doorstep.

Now, the living room. Once there he went to the windows at each end of the room, depositing the papers on the coffee table on the way past. The heavy drapes were pulled back and the tall shutters unlocked and folded away into their tall, narrow cupboards at each side of each window. Then he unlocked the door at the top of the stairs which went down to the servants' hall and kitchen, and took electric chair three. Down. More unlocking. The kitchen and servants' living room doors were unlocked, as were both the area and back doors, and the gate light extinguished, before he returned on the three-stage ascent on the electric chairs to his bathroom.

It was a long and tiresome routine — long enough for me to shave, shower and dress for the day ahead — but he performed it splendidly every morning undoing exactly what he had done so carefully the night before.

The bathroom was his last stop and the sound of running water was my cue to get down to the kitchen and start breakfast.

'Breakfast at eight-thirty,' Celia had said.

Kath, meanwhile, had reported to Mrs Beaumont and spent a good three-quarters of an hour preparing her for the day. It was slow work that required physical strength and patience from them both, especially the getting into and out of the old bathtub. The family had arranged the fixture of sturdy hand grips and rails at strategic spots around her bathroom but Mrs Beaumont could still manage to take only short, flatfooted, shuffling steps, even with the help of her walking frame. The time they spent together in this morning ritual seemed to tire them both. Once Mrs Beaumont was dressed Kath made the double bed and then left her in the bedroom to complete her personal toilet; Mrs Beaumont always came to breakfast with her hair done and a light touch of makeup.

At eight-twenty Mr Beaumont, dressed as if ready for The City, was in the living room, relaxing in an armchair with his paper. Meanwhile, left alone, Mrs Beaumont had finished her toilet. Then we heard the whine of the electric chair followed by the characteristic sounds of seat and arm being raised, and the thin, metallic banging of her aluminium walker muffled by its rubber feet and accompanied by a soft shuffling. It was a nervous time for us as she had to cross the hall over the loose rug which tended to gather up dangerously under her shuffling feet. Kath would hide at the bottom of the stairs waiting to run to her assistance if she fell but she always made the perilous crossing without incident.

Slowly and patiently she then made her way into the living room and down its length to the dining table. Her husband stood and helped her to her place at the table, pushing in the chair behind her. As they had separate bathrooms, and as Mr Beaumont did all his dressing in his so-called study — I never once saw him at work there — this was their first encounter of the day. Accordingly, a 'good morning, dear', and a 'good morning, darling', with a kiss to the cheek, were inevitable. Then he sat opposite her and together they checked the placement of the tableware, cutlery and condiments.

The table was always set the night before, Kath having established the breakfast menu with Mrs Beaumont as she cleared away after supper. But it had to be set perfectly even to the correct placement of the five toast spreads: the ginger marmalade and the orange marmalade had to be set out directly in front of Mr Beaumont's place, the strawberry jam and the honey directly in front of Mrs Beaumont's place, and the raspberry jam precisely between them in the middle of the table.

'Why?' I asked.

'I have no idea.'

Each of the five spreads was assigned its own little lidded pot. Each of these unpleasant little pieces of kitsch — for example, a china cottage with a removable 'thatched' roof and a spoon sticking out of the chimney for the strawberry jam, and a china beehive for the honey — had a different spoon and was assigned its own contents. It was an immutable arrangement. Furthermore, I had to empty, wash and refill them each day to ensure that the diners should not have to dig too deep into the container nor be offended by a dribble running down the edge. At first I had to make a written note of which sweet stuff went into which silly pot but I memorised it before long. Even so I was still somewhat nervous that I might do the refilling wrong. How, I wondered, would they ever cope with that?

So, providing all was well on the table the diners smiled at each other, arranged their napkins, and waited to be served.

And it was always exactly eight-thirty.

Chapter VIII

MARIANA, THE DAILY HOUSEKEEPER, ARRIVED FOR work each day at nine and stayed until about one-thirty. On Saturdays — ostensibly one of our days off — she replaced us for almost but not the entire day.

Dear Portuguese Mariana. She became our best friend. About my age, she was small and shapely, with olive skin, thick dark-brown hair, a flashing smile, sparkling black eyes and a predilection for clothes of black and red. She loved to sing and dance and drink wine and often spoke of the nights that she and her husband, Fabio, and their friends, spent dancing the *lambada*. Oh, how she loved to dance.

She and Fabio had lived in London for twenty-five years — longer than they had lived in Portugal — and her job at The Little Boltons was the only English work she had known. They were British citizens now, with two adult and very English children blessed with very English names. But even after twenty-five years Mariana still spoke English with a strong accent, an accent quite different from that of her Spanish friends.

Fabio was a commissionaire at a nearby international hotel. I saw him there sometimes and he looked dark and handsome in his gold-braided uniform, opening the door of a taxi in the forecourt. He, too, spoke with a strong and unusual accent, probably an asset in his job. Once, when we visited him and Mariana at home, he spoke directly to me, quietly and slowly, bringing his face close to mine, frequently touching my hand or arm with an intimacy that was very un-English.

'They good peoples,' he said, referring to the Beaumonts. He was in his armchair, enjoying a glass of wine and a cigarette, and he kept one eye on the Sky sports channel.

He leaned forward, put his flat hand to his chest. 'They good to us,' he whispered.

Then he closed his eyes and held his widely-spread fingers up to his forehead: 'But his brainis is going,' he said, and then relaxed back in his chair to take up his wine glass.

'He is old isn't it,' he added. 'Is okay, okay. We are like it if we live it that long.'

Fabio and Mariana were among the nicest, gentlest and most sincere people we had met and I wondered if the Beaumonts realised how lucky they were to have been served so well for so long by such a good person supported by such a good husband.

Poor, young and newly married, they had come to London from an impoverished inland village in Portugal seeking work. How Mariana got the job at The Little Boltons I didn't know but it coincided with the new Mrs Beaumont moving in and taking charge.

'Mrs Beaumont was such kind ladys to me all time,' Mariana said to me. 'But Mr Beaumont was not nice man. Me and Fabio live upstairis where you and Kat—' (she pronounced Kath as 'Kat', Bob as 'Bop') '—are living it and we have to stay there. Sometimes, at night, my little boy want to watch television but Mr Beaumont make us go upstairis. He wants to lock up everything downstairis. I no mind it but was not fair to my boy. He cry in bed very much.'

That explained something which had puzzled me. In the beginning we had tried passing our evenings in the same servants' downstairs living room to which Mariana was referring, watching television, reading, or writing letters, but stopped when Mr Beaumont, coming downstairs to make his nightly rounds to lock up the house and switch on the gate light, discovered us there and stopped to talk.

It was always a one-sided conversation, directed only at me, and it always took the same course.

'Been here nearly fifty years now you know. Like to lock up properly every night. Turn on the gate light. Can't help it. Fifty years. Have I shown you where to turn on the gate light?'

He had. Many times.

'Started off at Cheyne Court. Not this wife,' he continued. 'First wife. Died. Upstairs. In the bedroom. Bought the freehold after the war. Ministry of Food. Wales. Damned fool of a man, though. Good woman my wife. Can't get about like she used to. Damned pity. Got these electric chair affairs. Couldn't do without them. Here for the first wife I think.' (They weren't.) 'Can't remember. Damned nuisance. It's going. A Kentish man you know. That side of the Medway. Otherwise a man of Kent.'

The idea that the population of tiny Kent should be historically divided by a river into 'Kentish Men' and 'Men of Kent' — and that it mattered — astounded me. But it had to be true because I was told it so often.

'Clever little boy. Father sent me to—' here he paused for effect, lowering his head and looking over his glasses at me before carefully enunciating the name of his school, '—The Sir Joseph Williamson Mathematical School For Boys. Clever little chap. King's Scholar. Family not rich. Scholarship to King's School, Rochester, you know. Founded in six-hundred-and-four. Reconstituted by Henry the eighth — you know Henry the eighth? — '

I nodded.

'— in fifteen-forty-two. Prizes. Upstairs. Books. Never read them. Engraved.'

He indicated vaguely to 'our' television set playing in the corner; Kath was trying to watch it.

'Damned radio thing. Wife's watching it. Always on. Can't bear the noise. Can't see the point.'

Kath tried to relax during this nightly recitation but eventually, after hearing the same thing so often, we stopped using the living room at nights. I realised later, from what Mariana told us, that that was exactly what he wanted. He didn't want us lingering downstairs at night. He wanted to lock up everything as he had done slavishly every evening for nearly fifty years but as he couldn't drive us out by intimidation — as he once evicted Mariana and her little boy — he bored us out with his conversation.

'But why did you stay?' I asked Mariana.

'We have no money much,' she said. 'And where do we rent a flat in London? Is very expensive is it. We have to stay here until we have some monies. Fabio was very angry with Mr Beaumont. But now, he no mind it. Mr Beaumont likes Fabio now very much too I think it.'

Somehow, at some time, and with the help and support of her employers, Mariana and Fabio acquired a council flat on the King's Road. While only small it was obviously sufficient for the raising of their two children. And, as part of the Royal Borough, it was opulence itself compared with other disgraceful housing estates we had seen in the poorer boroughs of London. Interestingly, too, it had more comfort and luxury than the house in The Little Boltons, and was certainly furnished and decorated with more style. That would have been Mariana.

Mariana loved to talk to us. Despite her many years in London she still found the weather miserable and the winters unbearably cold. But it was her experience and belief that the price of a good income, and a better education for her children, was a harsh climate and a cool, unfriendly people. Conversely, and sadly, a warm climate, with warm people and an outdoor lifestyle, inevitably represented to her a peasant and subsistence existence. It surprised her, therefore, to hear about the antipodes.

'Mariana,' I told her. 'New Zealand is a small country, just like Portugal or England, but there are only three-and-a-half million people there. Compared with England, life is so easy. The weather is fine, especially in the north, and there is no pollution, no crowds. You could get a good job there. Things are cheap and you and Fabio could have a big house.'

'Oh,' she said, fascinated but unconvinced.

'Or you could go to Australia.'

I explained that Sydney, Melbourne and Brisbane were big, international cities overflowing with the people of southern Europe.

'The Australian climate is just like the Mediterranean,' I said, warming, as it were, to my subject. 'Like southern Europe. Better even. But there's more work. And life is so cheap compared to here.'

We had found that almost everything in England cost three times what it cost in New Zealand. And yet wages and salaries were usually about the same. No wonder Mariana and people like her found it so difficult.

'I like Portugal,' she said sadly. 'I wish we could afford to live there with our own peoples. But Portugal is a very poor country.'

'Brazil!' I said. 'In Brazil everyone speaks Portuguese. More people speak Portuguese in Brazil than there are people in Portugal.'

'Is a long way to Brazil,' she said. 'And Fabio doesn't like the aeroplaneis. I think we stay now in London. We go to Portugal for our holidaysis.'

Evidently she and Fabio had worked hard and saved enough to buy a condominium on the Algarve.

'We go there every year,' she said. 'I take English poundis and everythings is so cheap. We go to restaurantis every night and sit outside and is very beautiful and warm.

'But,' she said, resigned, 'we live London now. Is our home.'

Once Mariana's housekeeping duties had involved the entire house but now her hours had been reduced to part-time and so she busied herself only with those parts of the house still in use and therefore subject to inspection by her employer. After twenty-five years working in the old place she was wise enough to conserve her energy and do only what was necessary to keep Mrs Beaumont happy.

But not I. In the beginning I was determined to get the messy, and in parts dirty, kitchen into order. Each day I assigned myself a task to be completed after the morning dishes. Cupboards and drawers were emptied of anything that wasn't used which meant almost everything. I got rid of all the hotel-sized pots and pans, urns and tureens which had once been so new and shiny but were now only gathering grease and dust on the racks above the sink. I scoured the racks themselves back to their original condition. I delved deep into the pantry and food-storage cupboards discovering tins, jars and bottles of proprietary brands and labels from the nineteen-fifties. I threw out nothing but stored it all in the depths of the dark and tapering grotto, formed by the staircase, which was the redundant coal cellar.

I pulled out the range as far as its flexible gas pipe allowed and, using strong cleaners, cut through years of accumulated dusty grease on the surrounding tiles. I attacked the range itself, meticulously cleaning every knob and switch and chrome embellishment until the whole thing gleamed and sparkled as it must have done when new. I used a strong ammonia solution from the laundry to wipe over the entire kitchen paint-work sending myself dizzy in the process. Suddenly, though, a film of yellow was removed to reveal a clean and almost shiny painted finish beneath. I was elated, like the restorers of the Sistine Chapel, to discover the vivacity of the original light blue colour.

I was also elated to be so elated by something so simple. Brain rest, I decided, was good for me. And so was the physical effort.

I didn't need to do it; certainly neither Mr or Mrs Beaumont would ever know or notice it, but as I had to work there, and feed vulnerable old people from there, I thought I should make it as clean as possible.

'I am shamed you do this,' said Mariana. 'But this is the kitchen and—' and here she mentioned the name of the former Filipino cook, rolling her eyes in the process, '—doesn't let me work here. Is not my job she said it.'

'Don't worry, Mariana. I'm doing it because I want to.'

'Is very strange sometimes Bop,' she said to Kath out of my hearing.

Chapter IX

EACH MORNING BEFORE BREAKFAST, WHILE MR Beaumont was still upstairs, getting ready for the day, and Kath was still busy with Mrs Beaumont, I took the time to go outside, onto the street, to collect the milk and watch the world go by. I used the side door, which opened onto the area, and went up the brick steps that had looked so cold, dark, wet and forbidding on the day of our first visit. But it soon became familiar territory; our door to the outside world.

I liked The Little Boltons. It, the neighbouring The Boltons, and the adjacent streets and squares, were all built in the early eighteen-sixties on fields which had been owned and farmed by the Bolton family since the early sixteenth century. While the new houses were designed and built in a large and dignified style, the roads were then left rough and muddy. But history records that a wood-block pavement was laid in eighteen-eighty-four with a Macadam surface 'spread on the carriage road'. Of course it was all macadamised now, with cars parked, day and night, on both sides of The Little Boltons, but it was pleasant and quiet early in the morning.

The milkman — Tom — was always good for an early morning chat. He worked from a little green-and-white electric cart of the type I remembered from my childhood but long since abandoned in New Zealand. By catching Tom in the morning I could pick up last-minute items, from bread and eggs, cream and yoghurt, that I had forgotten to order the night before.

The milk crate was left at the top of the basement stairs beside the big, black, rubbery rubbish bins. Early one morning I lifted one of the rubbish bin lids to drop in something and found a woman's handbag and wallet. The handbag was ripped open and the wallet was empty of anything of value. But there was some identification. During the night a thief must have snatched the bag, emptied it of its cash, and taken the time to hide it in our rubbish bin. Instead of ringing the police immediately I left it until after breakfast; after all it was unlikely the thief would be hanging around waiting to get caught. Kath, meanwhile, casually mentioned the find to Mrs Beaumont and the affair was immediately taken out of our hands by Mr Beaumont.

The police were called and a couple of uniformed constables arrived more quickly than I expected. Apparently there had been a rash of bag snatching in the area and they were trying to get to the bottom of it. I found it odd, though, that although I had found the bag and discovered the name of the owner Mr Beaumont took charge of the whole affair. Unfortunately he knew nothing of the details, got everything wrong and gave the policemen completely erroneous information. This foolishness was due entirely to Mr Beaumont's idea that I was a servant and wouldn't or couldn't converse sensibly with members of the Metropolitan Police; in this the policemen themselves seemed to conspire. Not once, as I listened at the closed living room door, did I hear them ask such an obvious question as: 'Who actually discovered the bag, sir?' It seemed to me that to some people in England — including some police constables — intelligent servants simply didn't exist.

We received a lot of mail from home and my morning ventures outside gave me the opportunity to meet Peter the postman. One morning he proudly presented me with a small letter, with a New Zealand stamp, addressed in pencil in a large childish print that fell across the envelope:

the boltons of the little boltons
london
England

It was from a wee niece.

It seems Peter enjoyed the small joke of having a brace of Boltons living in his The Little Boltons; and the fact that we were New Zealanders, and thus spoke with a distinct accent, meant that I could meet him on the street and collect even un-numbered mail before he reached the house. He was not supposed to do it — to hand over the mail — but he knew that mail from New Zealand *had to* be ours. I collected the Beaumonts' mail at the same time.

'It's *not* mail, it's *post*,' Mr Beaumont insisted.

We discovered that getting to the mail (post) first was important when Mariana found a letter to us, from our accountant at home, in the wastepaper basket in the living room. It seemed that, unable to believe that servants would receive mail (post) of their own, especially from an international accounting firm, Mr Beaumont opened our mail (post) and then discarded the contents as obviously not for him.

Thus, if I didn't get our mail (post) directly from Peter in the morning we had to retrieve it later, opened, from Mr Beaumont's rubbish. I soon learned there was nothing I could do about this — it would be impossible to discuss it with him — but my annoyance was tempered knowing that Mariana checked the living room wastepaper basket for us each day.

Although we didn't meet many other people who lived in the street — they were generally an unfriendly lot probably sensing that we were servants — I did enjoy my conversations with Miss Tattersall, a neighbour, who was an exception. An elderly and independent lady, she was often out in the street in the morning, when I was, cleaning her Mini. She took great pride in the little old English thing having bought it new some years before. By nineteen-ninety-two, though, it was bent and dented and looking its age but she washed and polished it regularly and with great enthusiasm.

Oddly, though, whenever she cleaned the car she stripped down to her underwear — pants, bra and lacy petticoat — over which she wore a dirty old and oversized taupe-coloured raincoat, unfortunately buttoned only loosely. But she was friendly, if eccentric, and was always willing to stop and talk. She spoke with an accent so impossibly posh that at first I thought she was joking. And while not the slightest bit condescending, she nevertheless spoke to me as a servant, relating neighbourhood gossip that was servant-centred. Perhaps she thought that I had nothing else to talk about.

'Oh,' she said, pointing across the street with a hand full of cleaning rag, filthy, wet and dripping. 'That was the Onassis house once. Such a lovely man, you know.' She was referring not to anyone called Onassis but to the chauffeur. 'Took me to Sainsbury's once in his shooting brake.'

'Did he?' I said, encouragingly. 'In a shooting brake?'

Apparently the English of her class called all four-wheel-drive vehicles shooting brakes even if they were air-conditioned, turbo-charged, town-based luxury Range Rovers used only for driving to Sainsbury's.

'Oh, yes,' she said. 'Jolly big thing with big tires. So much snow, you know. Back in eighty-something. Couldn't get anywhere. Gave me a lift to the Cromwell Road.'

'Carlos and Maria live there,' she continued, pointing to another nearby house. She was referring to a Spanish couple who were servants to a resident lord. 'Been there for twenty-five years. Jolly nice people I think.'

When she was not on the street cleaning her car Miss Tattersall devoted herself to the welfare of Chelsea Pensioners. These inmates of the Chelsea Royal Hospital for old and disabled soldiers were often seen in the vicinity of the hospital and were recognisable by their comical scarlet jackets and black caps. Apparently she and her friends often took them, or some of them, on outings in and around London.

'Such dear chaps,' she said. 'And they do so love an outing.'

It was Miss Tattersall who told me how Mrs Beaumont used to get about so well in her own Mini.

'But she started bumping into walls and things you know. Had to stop driving after that. Such a dear lady.'

According to her, and as I had guessed, the Beaumont's used to entertain 'ever so much'.

'Always something going on at the Beaumont's in those days you know. Such a lovely, popular, social person. He'd be nothing without her, though,' she added. 'Nothing.'

She was shaking her head grimly as she spoke.

'Used to know a lady who was a secretary in The City,' she continued. 'Knew him, you know. Awful, hard man she said. Nobody could work for him.'

Well, I thought, I can. And do.

Like many such people Mr Beaumont had an unhealthy respect for authority of all kinds. Kath recognised that this was the problem with the nurses the family had employed in the past. Thinking it casual, part-time work, and glad to be out of a hospital, these intelligent and highly-qualified young women — inevitably from Australia or New Zealand — took to wearing jeans, sweatshirts and sneakers. To Mr Beaumont though they looked like mere schoolgirls who could have no authority over him in his own house.

'Get out!' he shouted bluntly if they tried to bathe him or help him dress, the very work for which they were employed. No wonder they didn't last long.

This changed remarkably, later, when it was necessary to employ a nurse again. Following Kath's advice she — a New Zealander from Napier — wore the semblance of a white uniform to look more like a real nurse. So attired, in the white weeds of a health professional, her nurse's badge pinned ostentatiously to her breast pocket, she found she could make her impatient patient do almost anything.

We had not been instructed to wear a uniform although I guessed our employers wished we would. But Kath intentionally wore combinations of black and white, in a near approximation of a maid's outfit, in order that Mr Beaumont could place her properly in his mind. He needed such signals to assign people their role in his life. The classless time in which he now found himself, in which rules and manners were not so fixed, were hard for him, and the presence of grandchildren, with their unisex dress, earrings, a hair length that was an unreliable guide to sex, and a relaxed attitude to life and other people, including him and us, confused him greatly.

The family had worried about how he would react to having a man in the kitchen and they were right: although he reluctantly accepted my presence he never got used to it and frequently came down to the kitchen just to see me at work. He would watch me curiously from the kitchen door, his eyes following my every move, as if to confirm a strange but unbelievable rumour. I didn't mind and sometimes tried to talk to him.

'Bally odd affair,' he said once. 'A man doing the cooking.'

'But the best chefs in the world are men,' I said, meaning to be jolly about it.

He looked at me fiercely.

'They're not men,' he said seriously, glaring at me over his glasses. 'They're French.'

Chapter X

MR BEAUMONT WAS ON A BREAKFAST FIBRE REGIME, ordered by the doctor for obvious reasons, comprising a grated carrot one morning and half a grapefruit the next. Actually he avoided fruit and vegetables whenever he could and tolerated this raw fibre start to the day only because it had been ordered by the doctor.

Celia had shown me how to prepare his morning carrot, coarsely grated and served in a small bowl. The result seemed unappetising to me so I grated it more finely, to release more of its juices, and added a few raisins and a generous dash of freshly squeezed orange juice. It looked nicer and tasted delicious.

Mr Beaumont professed to hate the juice of oranges and lemons — in fact he 'hated' a lot of things — but he didn't seem to notice the sweet juice I added to his carrot.

Half a grapefruit was deemed to satisfy his fibre needs every other morning. Seeking to provide only the best I chose the grapefruit myself, carefully picking over the barrows in the North End market looking for Californian or Floridian imports that were large, fresh, ripe and pink.

A special silver dish was assigned to carry the grapefruit half and it was my morning task to separate the segments and make them easy for Mr Beaumont to retrieve with his narrow spoon. I did my best, every second day, neatly scooping out each segment, ensuring that it completely detached from its little triangular home, before putting it back where it came from and garnishing the whole thing with a *glacé* cherry.

But I was doing it wrong.

'You're doing it wrong,' said Kath. 'He's complaining.'

'He's always complaining.'

'Well, he's complaining more about this.'

'Well how should I do it?'

'I don't know. All I know is that it's wrong.'

I tried everything. The problem was that whatever I was doing wrong was wrong not because it was wrong but because it was different from the way it had been done before. And Mr Beaumont couldn't explain to Kath how it should be done, how it was done before, because he simply didn't know. And while I was safe in the kitchen below — indeed I was rarely allowed above stairs — Kath had to wait table and take Mr Beaumont's complaints.

'I say,' he said to her once, pointing to the grapefruit half with his special spoon. 'This is just not right you know. Not right.' And then to his wife: 'Blasted colonials. Not that difficult you know.'

'Yes, darling,' replied Mrs Beaumont without looking up. 'Don't complain. I'm sure Bob's doing his best.'

Which I — the blasted colonial — was. But Kath was incensed by the 'colonial' business and was determined that we should get it right.

'What shall we do now then?' I asked.

'Try taking each bit out and removing all the stuff around it.'

'What?'

'The pith.'

'Pith off?'

'Yes!'

It was ridiculous. Two intelligent — if colonial — adults, equipped with various knives and spoons, hunched over a grapefruit half, discussing its dissection like consulting surgeons.

'Try it,' she insisted.

'I might as well chew the bloody thing for him. Then all he'd have to do is digest it.'

'Do it,' she said again. 'I'll help.'

So we did it. We removed all the little segments, one at a time, and laid them out on the work board in an exploded circle like a grapefruit pie chart. Then we took each one and gently peeled away its thin membrane.

'We're removing the stuff that does the job if you know what I mean,' I said.

'Who cares?'

'Not me.'

'Nor me.'

That operation complete we carefully replaced each naked little segment in its former position within the empty half skin.

'Here we go,' said Kath.

'Good luck,' I said.

But still it was wrong. And it was always wrong until Mariana — who knew what to do all the time — plucked up the courage to show me the correct procedure. It seemed she was intimidated by my kitchen 'skills' and couldn't believe I didn't know what to do.

'You are such a good cook, Bop,' she would say, especially when she was devouring my freshly-baked biscuits and cakes.

But now she could resist no longer.

'There is a knife,' she said, plunging her hand into a drawer that was as deep, dirty and dark as a gas-fitter's toolbox, and pulling out a strange little, curved and serrated stainless steel job. She wiped it on her apron.

'This is what is it you need,' she announced, in her unique and charming syntax, holding it up close to my face.

I'd never seen anything like it in my life. But she was right. It was exactly what I needed. Not because the finished work was any better than what I had accomplished on my own but because it was what Mr Beaumont was used to. He was happy at last. And so was Kath.

However, the alternating carrot/grapefruit regimen was his alone. Mrs Beaumont's fibrous needs were provided by a full glass of freshly squeezed orange juice which, together with the carrot or grapefruit, I prepared each morning.

In accordance with standing orders the orange was always de-juiced using a large and ungainly juice press of uncertain vintage called, imaginatively, an 'Instant' juice press which had a long, forward-curving, knob-ended handle that made it look more like a drill press than a kitchen tool. But it worked well, fiercely delivering plenty of fibrous material with the juice, although according to an advertisement I found, in a magazine from nineteen-thirty-five, the juice should have been clear and 'free of pips or pulp':

'Here's Health', it said.

> The splendid health-giving juice of oranges, lemons, grape-fruit, grapes, etc., is squeezed to the last clear drop with one stroke of the 'INSTANT' JUICE PRESS lever. Without pips or pulp it flows into your glass — quickly and simply. From all Ironmongers and Stores — strong and beautifully finished — price 20/-.

I prepared the morning's fibre — the first course — and loaded the dumb waiter in just the right order and with just the right plates, glasses, dishes and cups ready for serving.

Each meal required the use of its own allotted tableware and a set of plain white china was always used for breakfast; a beautiful green and gold *demi tasse* coffee set was used for the after-breakfast coffee.

Kath served the carrot (or grapefruit) and orange juice, which were consumed to the accompaniment of a light morning conversation which was reduced to a mere murmur as it drifted down to the kitchen through the hole in the floor created by the dumb waiter, now standing in the dining room, and returned to the kitchen. Meanwhile I prepared the main course. Grilled fish was often requested but I was disappointed never to be asked for kipper only because I want to see what this strange and uniquely English breakfast fish was like. Perhaps it was too working class for The Little Boltons.

But one popular fish request, for breakfast, was even stranger than kipper. When Kath first told me I thought she was joking.

'What?'

I couldn't believe it. I was juicing an orange at the time, for Mrs Beaumont, but I had to stop and sit down at the table.

'It's true. That's what she said.'

'I can't believe it.'

'It's what she wants.'

'A grilled sardine?' I still couldn't believe it.

'Yes.'

'Out of one of those little tins full of oil? With a key?'

'Yes.'

'One oily sardine each?'

'Yes.'

'On toast.'

'Yes. No. Grilled on toast.'

'Grilled on toast?'

'Yes.'

'Are you sure?'

'Yes. That's what she said.'

Even Kath, who tried hard to defend Mrs Beaumont's tastes, was bursting to laugh. And we both did laugh, aloud, and found it hard to stop when, after only a few seconds under the grill, we solemnly laid out the tiny, shiny, silvery, oily, headless little creatures on their own little slices of brown toast.

Usually, though, the preferred breakfast, if not ordinary grilled fish, was lightly scrambled or soft boiled eggs, and always followed by coffee. And it all had to be ready precisely when required as neither delay nor overcooking was tolerated.

After the fibre course Kath cleared the table and sent the dumb waiter down to the kitchen. I emptied it and loaded it with the main course. With everything ready and in place I hit the button that sent it all up to the dining room. Meanwhile Kath, somewhat revived by a quick cup of tea I always had ready for her, and perhaps a slice of toast, rushed upstairs to meet the rising main course and begin serving.

Toast was required hot so bread and toaster stayed upstairs and it was Kath's job to supervise the toasting and serve the first rounds. She then returned to the kitchen to finish her own breakfast. As soon as she knew, from the sounds above, that the upstairs breakfast was over she returned to the dining room and loaded the soiled dishes onto the dumb waiter and sent them down to me again. I, below, replaced them with the fresh coffee, ready for serving, and sent the mad machine up on its return journey.

Now, upstairs, all was quiet. Mr and Mrs Beaumont sat in the living room enjoying their coffee and newspapers, blissfully unaware of the heat and chaos below stairs. His paper, predictably perhaps, was *The Times*, hers, *The Independent*, an unconventional choice — according to the newsagent one of the few of that title required in the street — but it seemed appropriate to her, as if purposely chosen to reflect her own independent spirit.

So they read and it was an hour or so before they stirred. Then Mrs Beaumont shuffled off with her walker to her ground floor study where she worked on her correspondence and household affairs before having the regular morning meeting with Kath. At this meeting she sat at her desk in her wheelchair while Kath sat forward on a chair to her left as they discussed the coming day, the coming week, what special chores were required, who might be calling for 'tea', and, especially, the day's menu and what had to be ordered or bought for the kitchen. Kath then came back down to the kitchen to give me the instructions which determined the course of my day.

While Mrs Beaumont phoned many of the suppliers herself — she seemed to be on personal terms with most of them — to order what was required for delivery, I could buy most of what she ordered for a fraction of the price at nearby Sainsbury's. But we realised that she may never have been to a modern supermarket and was therefore unaware of either the wide range of products available or the savings that could be made.

Chapter XI

THE COLOSSAL CONTRAPTION OF A DUMB WAITER, which we came to call The Monster, was essential to the efficient working of the kitchen. Indeed, Kath — or any kitchen maid of the past — could never have managed to do what The Monster did so easily: carry full and empty plates to and from the dining room above many times during every meal.

The vertical framework of The Monster was wood. Two immense brown-varnished timbers, set into the concrete floor against the wall in one corner of the kitchen, rose majestically to the ceiling, stopping short of breaking into the room high above. Instead, the running arms of the waiter itself — a doorless, two-shelf cupboard affair — were so designed beneath it that they carried the waiter up ahead of them. It, the waiter, then collected the green carpeted floor hatch on its top as it passed through the floor where it — the carpeted floor hatch — rested for the duration. To someone standing in the dining room, therefore, the waiter appeared to emerge miraculously through the floor, carrying a little square of carpet on its head, to stand there, without apparent support, for as long as necessary. When it was returned below it slipped out of sight leaving the floor hatch to drop noiselessly into its correct position in the floor.

The mechanical engineering of The Monster was a model of Heath Robinson ingenuity. Thick steel cables, black with grease, ran up, down, around and through a series of spinning cast-iron wheels and pulleys in a manner designed to lighten the load. Meanwhile a heavy iron counterweight ran up and down in its own greasy wooden slot against the wall.

The gearing was originally very low presumably because the assumed motive power was a frail kitchen maid turning a handle on a black iron wheel. But sometime after the reticulation of electricity a heavy-duty electric motor had been installed. This innovation obviously presented the engineers of the time with an entirely new challenge. Accordingly, a flywheel was installed, together with even more reducing gears and cables, all designed to compensate for the electric motor's vast power and speed.

A simple switching mechanism in the kitchen, and a matching one in the dining room, was all that was required. Red was up, green was down; to press was to deliver power, to cease pressing was to cut power. Accurate timing was important if the waiter was to come to rest in the correct and most convenient position. To continue pressing when it was at the extreme end of its run in either direction was to risk blowing a fuse. We blew a few fuses but it was always a quick and easy job to replace them and get The Monster moving again.

But one fateful day The Monster stopped mid-journey and would not re-start. Its top half, complete with its carpet-square hat, comically poked half-way up through the dining room floor while something in the motor slipped and whirred, sending out clouds of acrid smoke.

Obviously this was serious. So Fergus, the 'do-anyfing' handyman employed for household maintenance and repairs, was duly called.

'The motor's gawn,' said Mickey, the electrician who worked for Fergus.

'Watcha mean gawn?' asked Fergus.

They were both on their knees in the corner of the kitchen inspecting The Monster's motor while The Monster itself remained suspended menacingly above them. I was standing, watching, anxious not only to get on with my work but also that they should fix it quickly. Kath was finding it exhausting to carry everything up and down stairs at every meal.

'Burnt art. Blarn up. Gawn f'rever.'

'Carn't be fixed then?'

'Nah,' said Mickey. 'S'too old innit. Godda gedda noo one.'

'I'll tell the guv'nah.'

They straightened up but they were still kneeling.

'S'bleedin' diabolical, innit,' said Mickey.

Mickey loved to say 'diabolical'.

'Wha' is?'

'The bleedin' wiring. S'chronic.'

Mickey loved to say 'chronic', too.

'Dunno, Mickey,' said Fergus. 'You're the bleedin' expert incha? Can ya fix it?'

'Nah,' said Mickey. 'Too dangerous. But I'll make it bedda when we do the motor.'

'Bedda? Hah?'

'I'll pu' a switch at the top, a switch at the bottom, and I'll make the fing stop automatic,' he said. 'Easier on the motor, too.'

'Clever geezer incha,' said Fergus with a wink to me.

So for the next couple of weeks, on and off, Mickey spent his time fixing The Monster and making it 'bedda'. Once a new motor was purchased its installation took no more than half a day. The rest of the time was spent rewiring. It was a complicated process because Mickey wanted the waiter to be sent either up or down from either upstairs or downstairs. And he wanted to arrange a switching device in each direction that turned the motor off at precisely the right time when The Monster was in precisely the right place so it would never again fuse. Getting that right alone took much experimentation especially as he seemed to be making up the plan as he went along. Thus we became used to sudden and loud bangs, and clouds of electrical smoke, as 240 dangerous volts objected loudly and violently to what he was trying to make them do.

Meanwhile the household had to function as usual which was less than simple without The Monster. At some time in the past the winding handle had been disengaged, presumably in the interests of user safety, so Mickey had engaged it again to raise and lower The Monster by hand as required.

The first time I did it Kath was upstairs for lunch.

'Oh, yes,' said Mr Beaumont, seeing the green-hatted thing emerge silently from below. 'Much better. Quiet. Good chap that Fergal. Good chap.'

He called Fergus Fergal and Mickey Mike.

Mickey was visited by Fergus at least once a day.

'Gawd 'elp us, Mickey,' he said every day. "Ow long's it gunna take nah? The guv'nah's getting the 'ump.'

Despite the inconvenience I enjoyed having Mickey about the kitchen. And when Fergus turned up each day I enjoyed listening to them speak in their native cockney, an accent as lyrical, colourful, inventive and authentic as any in the world. For example during the course of their conversations they often talked of a colleague I'd never met they called 'haitch'.

'Why do you call him haitch?' I asked, innocently.

'Because he's got diabolical hackney,' they said as if it was the most obvious answer in the world.

But Fergus and Mickey's lively wit, and their apparent inability to deal with some of the English language's most common sounds, masked a breadth of education and experience, and depth of intelligence, which they seemed intentionally to conceal. It was as if they realised that in houses like this, probably typical of their customer list, the tradesmen were assumed to be humorous oafs with working class accents. But while Fergus and Mickey were certainly humorous, they were definitely not oafs, and they were working class only because their work was manual and because in England everyone has to belong to a class.

Mickey was an electrical aeronautical engineer. While qualified to work on aeroplanes he seemed satisfied to work with or for Fergus, carrying a bag of tools around London by tube to wherever he was sent from his home somewhere up the 'Norvern Line'.

'Why?' I asked. 'With your skills you could work anywhere in the world.'

'Nah,' said Mickey, pushing his long hair back out of his eyes and looking up at me from where he crouched on the kitchen floor. 'Don' like the work. Too much bovver. An' all that noise. Not healfy.'

And when he looked at me directly, and added with surprising sincerity: 'I belong 'ere in London, know wha' I mean?' I knew exactly what he meant.

Fergus was a plumber; it was a useful trade which he had plied all over the world. He knew New Zealand and Australia well having travelled and worked there for some years. He'd also travelled throughout Asia and the United States. As a result he had a broad view of the world and was one of the few tradesmen who visited the house who had any sense of how strange London must have seemed to us.

'Watcha wanna work 'ere for?' he asked, arms crossed, leaning against the stove, chatting.

'It's different,' I said. What else could I say?

'Bleedin' different's righ',' he said, rolling his eyes.

We saw a lot of Fergus, especially in the winter. Before our arrival he had been responsible for the installation of the new gas-fired water-heating system which not only supplied hot water to the kitchen and bathrooms but also moved it through a complex of ancient pipes to the heating radiators installed in each room. The complete apparatus of copper and brass, made even more intricate because the water needed to be softened by salt — so mineral deposits wouldn't build up and clog the system — and kept separate from the drinking water, was installed in the laundry.

A confusing network of pipes, in and out, coded red and green, was reproduced on a plan pasted to the adjacent wall. But it made no sense to me. It looked like an expensive installation and was, as far as I could tell, an exceedingly tidy and professional job.

Not so, however, with the radiators themselves. Antiquated, over-painted, cast-iron, skeleton-like beasts, they stood against the wall in each room collecting dust around their feet and radiating heat in a most primitive manner. And they frequently didn't work.

'The guv'nah's barmy,' said Fergus. 'He spends farsands o' parns fixing the boiler and won't replace the old radia'ors.'

Obviously it was a false economy because in our winter there most of the radiators had to be replaced, one at a time. Until they were, however, there were frequent problems with air in the pipes.

'They need bleedin',' said Fergus, for once using the word as it was meant to be used. 'I'll show ya what to do.'

It was a simple process using a special radiator key — a rad key he called it — to open a valve on top of the radiator and allow the trapped hot air to be pushed out by the pressure of the rising water. One had only to be sure that the valve was closed again before hot water was sprayed into the room.

It was an old-fashioned heating system, working on rudimentary principles that were easy to understand. But my expertise with the rad key was considered a remarkable achievement by the owner of the house, resident there for nearly fifty years. It saved him calling

Fergus every time there was a bleeding problem and for that alone he congratulated himself for employing such a practical and versatile manservant: me.

Chapter XII

AS EACH MEAL PROGRESSED I WASHED THE DISHES — mostly by hand — as Kath cleared them from the table and sent them down to me on The Monster. There was a dishwasher but it was an early model — at least forty years old, surely one of the oldest in use at that time — and it was virtually useless. The racks were almost rusted through and regardless of how hard and how much I cleaned it there was always a suspicious scum on the water and an especially unpleasant-looking deposit on the dishes it was supposed to have cleaned.

Before long I decided that a replacement was essential. I was sure Mrs Beaumont had no idea of the old dishwasher's condition nor that I was washing all the dishes by hand. She appreciated whatever we did for her and was always plain and straightforward to deal with. But there were some things with which she would not or could not concern herself, deferring to her husband, and the problem dishwasher was one.

My relationship with Mr Beaumont was fluid and unpredictable, changing almost daily, depending more on how he felt than on what I did. Knowing that a quick dishwasher decision was impossible I worked cunningly on the matter for a couple of weeks. Whenever he was downstairs, for whatever reason, I raised the subject, each time from a different angle, hoping I would either convince him through argument or wear him down with persistence. Sometimes I even managed to coax him into the body of the kitchen. I opened the dishwasher door and showed him how old and rusted the inside of the cabinet was. He put one hand on the top and leaned over stiffly, with one counterbalancing leg sticking out behind, and looked inside and then up to me as if looking for some guidance. I realised then that the insides of this particular forty-year-old dishwasher were the only dishwasher insides he had ever seen, that he had never looked inside it before, and that he had no idea what he should be looking at or for.

'Wife bought it,' he said. 'Forty years. Still going. Good show.'

'But, Mr Beaumont. It is very old. It doesn't work anymore. It needs replacing.'

He looked at me over his glasses with amazement.

'Rubbish,' he shouted and walked away.

I asked Fergus for his opinion.

'Have you ever seen a dishwasher like this before?'

'Give ova,' he said. 'Neva seen nuffing like it in all me bleedin' days.'

'Never?'

'Neva. S'old innit. S'older 'n me. S'old as the bleedin' 'ills.'

'Would it be worth anything as a trade-in?'

'Wurf a bleedin' forchune,' he said, 'in the Bri'ish Museum.'

'I'm going to get him to buy a new one.'

'Brave incha,' said Fergus with a wink. 'Guv'nah's not gunna buy a noo one. Betcha.'

'What about the washing machine and drier?' I said. The washer and drier were new machines purchased only weeks before our arrival. 'They're new.'

'The missus's family bough' 'em. Caused a bleedin' stink then an' all.'

'Well I'm going to get him to buy a new one.'

'If 'e buys a noo one,' said Fergus confidently, hands on hips, 'then I'll install it and take away the old one for nuffing.'

And sell it to the British Museum, I thought.

I spent an afternoon at Peter Jones's in Sloane Square, getting all the prices and comparisons for suitable machines. With the assistance of a helpful salesman I settled on the ideal and most affordable model and obtained a firm price. And then eventually, with Kath talking to Mrs Beaumont, and Mrs Beaumont presumably talking to Mr Beaumont, I got Mr Beaumont to agree.

Amazing.

'But how shall I pay?' I asked.

'Harrods. Selfridges, Peter Jones,' he said. 'All of them. I have an account.'

'Oh. Well I got this price at Peter Jones.'

'Decent firm. Arrange it, then. Telephone them dammit. Charge it. Good show.'

So I telephoned the salesman and ordered the dishwasher, giving Mr Beaumont's full name and address. But nothing happened. So I phoned the Peter Jones salesman again.

'I phoned back,' he said.

'You did?'

'Yeah. I did.'

I knew the problem. Receiving telephone calls was impossible. Mr Beaumont didn't allow servants to use the phone so if there were a call for one of us he would simply hang up.

'I spoke to Mr Beaumont.'

'And what's the problem?'

'He doesn't have an account here. Never has done.'

'Never?'

'Never. So we'll need a cheque. I told him.'

I gave up.

'Tol'ja, didn't I,' said Fergus.

I continued to use the old dishwasher for some of the dishes — I had no choice — but I continued to wash the fine china, crystal and silverware by hand in a late attempt to save them from the corrosive effects of dishwashing detergents. But it was almost futile because former employees had not known nor cared what damage could be done to materials never designed to withstand the chemical rigours of a dishwasher; and Mrs Beaumont didn't seem to notice their deteriorating condition. And that left only the cooking ware which the old machine couldn't clean anyway.

'Let me be the first to welcome the Boltons of The Little Boltons to our little library,' said the lady librarian when we joined the Old Brompton Library. I enjoyed doing research there and from my reading of the history of The Little Boltons, originally named The Grove, I learned that during the eighteen-sixties one house in the area had employed five people below stairs: a butler, a cook, two housemaids and a nurse, as well as the coachman and his family who lived in the mews above the stables. But whether five house servants (and a coachman and his family) were typical I couldn't be sure as I found that another house in the street had boasted a below-stairs staff of nine.

While once I would have wondered how one house — even a large house — could have kept all those servants fully occupied I now realised that there could be no shortage of work in a house where high standards could be met only through manual labour. Even at The Little Boltons in nineteen-ninety-two Mariana could do only so much in a large, old and dusty house. And doing the laundry and the ironing for just two old people, even with the help of a new automatic washer and drier — which Mr Beaumont called 'those damned newfangled gadgets' — kept both her and Kath busy for hours of most days. It wasn't even Kath's job to help in the laundry but it was obvious that without her help Mariana would have been overwhelmed.

The laundry room had a concrete floor that sloped to a drain in the middle. As well as the new washer, drier, ironing board and iron, it was furnished with old concrete tubs and, in a direct link to the past, a trapeze-like arrangement that hung from the ceiling. It was an elaborate contraption of wooden frames, bleached and worn furry from use, strung with a complex of cords and pulleys in such a way that the frames could be raised and lowered as required. It was used, as in the Dickensian past, for hanging the damp laundry during the ironing and before being stored. It looked awfully primitive and I felt sorry for the poor laundry maids who once must have had to manage it on their own.

Apart from our own laundry, which went from machine to machine and back to our room on the same day, the household washing, especially sheets, pillow cases, tablecloths and table napkins, had to be ironed by hand in accordance with Mrs Beaumont's instructions. The objective seemed to be a tidy look to the basement linen cupboards (into which she never looked) and, later, a neat and square symmetry on bed, pillow or table. That meant folding everything with perfect geometry and ironing with sharp edges and no double-creases. And because everything was old heavy-duty cotton — Mrs Beaumont seemed unaware of modern, blended, no-iron materials — it had to be ironed the old-fashioned way: wet. Hence the elevated wooden racks still served their purpose, even for Kath and Mariana, of holding the heavy wet sheets off the floor while they were being ironed and then carrying them high above, out of the way, where they could be left to dry in the air. I suppose the fact that these ancient sheets and pillow cases were still in use was a credit to the English mills which once made them. But it did mean an extraordinary amount of unnecessary work that modern housekeepers simply wouldn't tolerate.

Even Mr Beaumont's shirts and elephantine underpants had to be ironed wet in this way. Luckily, said Kath, he changed each of them only once a week. The bed linen, though, was changed much more often — sometimes for the most unfortunate reason — and a good supply had to be kept ready in the warming cupboard behind the furnace.

One night — or rather in the early hours of one morning — we were rudely awakened by the harsh electric bell installed for emergencies above Kath's bed. It was part of a servant-summonsing bell system that had once been wired throughout the house but was now alive only in the kitchen and our bedroom. Mrs Beaumont kept a bell-push beside her bed; obviously something was wrong.

Struggling out of sleep, and expecting the worst, we then heard Mr Beaumont's calling plaintively from the bottom of the stairs.

'I say. Bolton! Bolton!'

Reacting more quickly than Kath, I threw on my robe and went to our landing. Without an electric chair up to our floor Mr Beaumont was reduced to calling up to us in this way. I saw him standing two landings below, wearing his white towelling robe, shading his eyes from the light I had switched on.

'What is it? Is Mrs Beaumont all right?'

By now Kath was behind me.

'Mrs Bolton,' he said to Kath, ignoring me. 'I'm afraid the wife's had a bit of an accident.'

He looked helpless and confused. I felt the same.

Kath ran down to their bedroom while he, relieved, retired to his study to wait. I, too, waited, hoping Mrs Beaumont was all right but unwilling to follow Kath into the privacy of their bedroom. Before long, though, she returned.

'God,' she said, annoyed rather than concerned. 'Could you come and give me a hand?'

'What's the matter?'

'I have to remake the whole bed.'

'Why? Has she wet it?'

'Well, sort of.'

'What do you mean? '

'Her hot water bottle. It's leaked everywhere. The bed's saturated.'

'Oh. You couldn't have made it tight enough.'

'I *did* make it tight enough. The thing's so old it's perished.'

'Didn't you notice?'

'No.'

'*I* would have noticed.'

'Well *you* tuck her into bed every night if you're so smart. And give her a bath and empty her commode. I'll do the cooking. That's easy.'

'Easy!'

We were both angry. Not at each other but from being wakened from our so-much-needed sleep. But then Kath laughed at our silliness.

'Come on,' she said. 'Let's get it over with.'

And so, while she stripped the bed of its wet sheets, and turned the heavy mattress on her own, I trudged down the five flights of stairs to the warming cupboard far below in which an unlimited store of clean sheets, so carefully washed and precisely ironed and creased, lay white and waiting for just such an occasion. Then we remade the bed together, working one each side, while Mr and Mrs Beaumont sat in a chair, one each side of the room, watching us at our nocturnal work.

Back in our own room, depressed that we had only a few hours of darkness left before we had to be up again, Kath tried to make the most of it.

'Well at least it was only water,' she said. 'It could have been worse.'

And sometimes it was.

Chapter XIII

MRS BEAUMONT LIKED TO GO OUT BEFORE LUNCH. The family was right: she was in desperate need of outside stimulation but without willing or understanding staff she had been left to her own resources in the house. We knew how difficult that must have been for her. Even confined to her chair most of the time she was bright and alert. She read the papers from front to back, watched all the television news, disapproved of the royal scandals, kept up with politics, sports — she loved Wimbledon — and the theatre. And she loved to talk about it all to Kath.

Her deafness meant that a real conversation was not easy but Kath did learn from her that she had, like Kath, written children's books — but what books? — and she had somehow been involved in the promotion of the Indian film industry — how? — with a zeal that had been recognised with an O.B.E. She had travelled throughout western Europe and the then communist eastern Europe and, so far as Kath could tell, throughout much of Asia and most of north Africa. But how? And why? Kath learned only so much and could not draw her on any details.

And then, later of course, she and Mr Beaumont had taken three — not two, as Mr Beaumont had told me, but three— round-the-world cruises on the Canberra. They were expensive jaunts too as I once found an old Canberra advertising brochure from which I could deduce, from what Mrs Beaumont had told Kath about their deck and cabin positions, that they must have paid about fifty thousand pounds for at least one of the trips, probably the last, in nineteen-ninety.

But despite having had such a busy life, seeing so much of the world, and having so much money, Mrs Beaumont was modest and unassuming and simply didn't care to talk about herself, her travels or the past. But she did love to go out, and once she discovered that Kath was a willing pusher the morning wheelchair ramble became a permanent feature of the daily routine.

A succession of servants and nurses unwilling or reluctant to push an old lady about the streets in a wheelchair meant that before we arrived Mrs Beaumont had managed to get out of the house only rarely. And even when she was able to cajole the nurse *du jour* into a walk, the reluctant pusher, eager to be done with the tiresome and tiring task, would race Mrs Beaumont along thus defeating the purpose of the outing and scaring the old dear witless in the process. The result — perhaps the desired result from the pusher's point of view — was that Mrs Beaumont lost her enthusiasm, even her nerve, for walks, and had stopped asking.

Kath believed her reluctance was understandable; for someone accustomed to moving at only a shuffle pace to be suddenly hurtling along ahead of a brisk young walker, with no means of control, sitting helpless and unrestrained in a wheelchair designed for the indoors, must have been a terrifying experience. Aware of her terror, and yet knowing how trapped the uncomplaining lady must have felt without her walks, Kath made it clear that she would always be happy to go out. And when Mrs Beaumont discovered that Kath understood both her need for outings and that the distance covered was less important than the time taken, it didn't take her long to regain her confidence. Before long they were going out almost every morning, not returning until lunch.

Once she and Kath finished their morning meeting in the study, and Mrs Beaumont completed whatever other household business was necessary there — and providing only that it wasn't snowing, hailing or raining heavily — it was my job to get the wheelchair outside and down onto the front path. Kath and I together then helped Mrs Beaumont down the few stairs, slowly, one at a time, until, almost exhausted from the effort, she flopped heavily into the chair. Now, as she adjusted herself for maximum comfort, she began to look around, bright-eyed and full of anticipation, conscious of the weather for the first time.

But such was her pleasure from her outings that the state of weather rarely bothered her. If it were cold she wrapped herself in a heavy coat inside which she clutched a hot water bottle, donned sheepskin-lined boots, and lay a woollen rug across her lap. Even on wet mornings she stayed indoors more out of consideration for Kath than from an aversion to the elements.

When at last she was ready, and with shopping bag hooked over the back of the chair, off they went, this way or that. I stood at the gate, watching for a few minutes, and was not surprised to see them stop only two or three houses away. I could see Mrs Beaumont reaching out of the chair to grasp the leaf of a plant between her thumb and fingers, feeling its texture. And Kath, with a firm grasp on the chair's rubber hand-grips, leaning forward to listen to what Mrs Beaumont had to say. Then they moved off again and I watched, amused, to see the old arms out now to the left, now to the right, as she pointed out something of local interest.

In this way, with Kath going as slowly as possible, they ambled around the streets, squares and gardens of the neighbourhood which had been Mrs Beaumont's home for twenty-five years. Many stops were made to look at house gardens in particular but also to discuss the history of this house or that, and some item of past gossip about former residents and friends. Thus we learned where Lord This and Lady That lived, where — in Colherne Court at the end of the street — a young Lady Diana Spencer had once lived, the house which (as Miss Tattersall had already told me) once belonged to the Onassis family, which house was being renovated by Mark Thatcher, the prime minister's son, and why a mansion in The Boltons, the next street, the London home of some or other Middle Eastern potentate, was always boarded up.

Brompton Cemetery was nearby and a walk through its tree-lined lanes was always appreciated. Mrs Beaumont had an uncle from an ancient line of Scots aristocracy buried there, as well as a family vault. She once asked Kath to work with the curator to determine whether, when the time came, there might be room therein for this particular family member. It was a strange duty — which Kath was required to perform secretly — and not one that she willingly assumed; but after making some only cursory enquiries Kath quietly allowed the matter to drop and Mrs Beaumont never raised it again.

Mrs Beaumont enjoyed the tranquillity of the cemetery. She knew of so many interesting, famous and historical figures buried there that she frequently urged Kath to leave the marked path in search of something more interesting that was, literally, off the beaten track. It was especially difficult for Kath, who found the chair-pushing taxing enough on level and paved streets, but they pressed on bravely, down rough avenues of soft earth, rank grass and weeds, rising tree roots and broken headstones. It was not only hard work for Kath it was also dangerous for Mrs Beaumont but she seemed unaware of the risks having acquired an unreasonable faith in her pusher's strength and stamina.

'God, I nearly lost her today,' said Kath on one occasion.

She was standing, shivering, in the kitchen with the fingers of one hand hooked into muddy shoes, an almost-cold hot water bottle in the other hand, telling me how her teamster had driven her deeper and deeper into the wilds of Brompton Cemetery.

'Where did you go?'

'Right off the main path towards Finsborough Road.'

Mrs Beaumont had demanded that Kath leave the footpath to follow an unpaved track leading up to a raised terrace.

'We had to go along this terrace to find the grave of some famous botanist or other,' said Kath. 'I don't know who it was but she knew what she was looking for.'

'Did you find it?'

'Oh, yes. At last. But she had no idea how hard it was for me. Or how dangerous it was for her.'

Evidently the raised track was so narrow that it was impossible for Kath to turn the wheelchair around and so she had to return to the main path pulling the wheelchair backwards.

'In the end it wasn't so much hard as scary,' she said nervously. 'I was so frightened. I mean, she could have fallen out so easily; then what would I have done? It's so lonely in there.

'She showed me the grave of Emmeline Pankhurst,' she added, almost as an afterthought.

During his wife's absence Mr Beaumont was irritable, even jealous, padding around the room impatiently like a caged lion waiting for his lunch. He had no interest in going out himself — except for a regular Thursday outing — preferring to remain in the living room all morning, dressed in his three-piece suit and tie. He spent his time dozing, staring into space, and trying to talk to

Mariana over the sound of the Hoover. Kind Mariana. She stopped the Hoover, stood up the handle, and sat down with him, grateful, I suppose, for the break.

'I was a clever little boy you know, Mariana,' he said as he did most days.

She came down to join me in the kitchen, laughing but not unkindly.

'He ask me if I was knowing his mother,' she said. 'I said: 'Mr Beaumont, I'm not that old.

'Poor Mr Beaumont,' she added sadly.

'He's lazy, Mariana,' I said. 'He doesn't go out. He has no one to talk to. He does nothing. He's not interested in anything. Old people have to keep their bodies and minds active to stay healthy.'

Mariana leaned on her broom and looked thoughtfully out the window at the sick bay tree.

'Mr Beaumont is a very healthy strong man I think it,' she said at last. 'But I worry about his brainis. He is forget everything. Fabio thinks it too.'

She paused and looked at me with her large black eyes.

'I think Mrs Beaumont is worried. In here—' she tapped her chest '—is worried. Sometimes, when he says funny thingis I see her look at him sad.'

Mariana looked at me sad, in sympathy. Suddenly I, too, felt sad. I had to shake myself out of it.

'He's all right, Mariana. He's harmless. And he likes you.'

I found it hard to dislike Mr Beaumont. Rather, I felt sorry for him. And, yes, a bit sad for him; so narrow in his experiences and outlook; so constrained by his routine.

'I know it,' Mariana continued, occasionally sweeping at nothing. 'Even when he was rude to me I no mind it. I know Mr and Mrs Beaumont twenty-five yearis. I know them very well. And I know his brainis is going.'

'Is he rude to you sometimes?'

'Is rude not now,' she said with a dismissive wave of her free arm and a shrug of her shoulders. 'But twenty-five yearis, when I come to London from Portugal with Fabio and my baby, we live here, where you and Kath are upstairis, and he was very rude man to me. I cry many times.'

This about the cantankerous but harmless old man who was waiting upstairs so impatiently for his wife and mine to return from their walk.

Chapter XIV

BROMPTON CEMETERY WASN'T THE INTREPID wheel-chair walkers' only destination; sometimes they went much farther afield and for all sorts of reasons.

One afternoon, while she was helping Mrs Beaumont after her rest, Kath found her scratching around in her drawer for perfume. She had several little bottles but they were all empty or almost empty.

'I would love some new perfume, dear,' she said by way of explanation.

Evidently she enjoyed having a variety of perfumes available but had to rely on her family to choose something when gift-giving was appropriate. Kath suggested, therefore, that on one of their morning walks they should go to Boots on the King's Road. She suggested that shop because she knew that as well as having a large perfume department it had a street-level access and was laid out with aisles wide enough to easily accommodate the wheelchair. She didn't want to cause a traffic jam.

'Oh, no, dear,' said Mrs Beaumont. 'That's much too far for you to push.'

During the afternoons which followed Kath again observed the struggle Mrs Beaumont had to obtain even a drop of perfume. She suggested the walk to King's Road again and again.

'Perhaps one day. When it's fine.'

As she enjoyed her walks so much, and as she obviously needed the perfume, Kath couldn't understand the reason for her reluctance. Whatever it was, though, it was eventually outweighed by her shortage of perfume and the anticipation of being able to make her own choice. Thus, on one especially fine day, when Kath again made the suggestion, she agreed.

Actually, as Kath remembered it later, she didn't exactly agree. She didn't say 'no' but she didn't quite say 'yes' either preferring for some reason to leave the decision and the responsibility to Kath. Kath guessed that part of the problem was that the extra distance required an outing of longer duration than usual. She also knew that not only did Mr Beaumont resent his wife's absences but that the rigid observance of the timetable for luncheon and pre-lunch drinks was important to them both.

'We must be back in time for lunch though, dear.'

Accordingly they cut short the morning study meeting and left half-an-hour earlier than usual. Instead of the customary ritual, with my getting the wheelchair down to the path and Kath and Mariana fussing about over Mrs Beaumont's warmth and comfort, Kath ensured that the process of leaving was conducted without fuss or delay. This more businesslike approach to the morning lasted, by agreement, all the way to Boots. This, they both knew, was not an occasion for aimless strolling and garden appreciation. This was a journey with a purpose. A mission. To get the perfume. And get home. In time for lunch. And the drinks that should precede it.

It was to the very fashionable part of King's Road they were heading. Kath had checked the map carefully, plotting the shortest possible route. Even so it was a good few kilometres; an easy stroll for her on her own but how long would it take pushing a heavy old lady in a small-wheeled wheelchair not meant for the outdoors.

Crossing Fulham Road she cut through to King's Road as soon as she could but by the time she reached it she knew there was still a long way to go. It was taking her longer than she expected so she hurried, as carefully as she could, wanting to give Mrs Beaumont as much time as possible in the shop.

They reached the busier and more fashionable neighbourhood where the footpath was clogged with slow-moving pedestrians. So, taking a big breath, Kath began dodging and weaving the wheelchair, looking for gaps in the crowd, and going at such a pace that people had to jump out of her way.

They got to Boots in just over forty-five minutes.

'I knew then that we'd be another three-quarters-of-an-hour getting home,' Kath said later. 'What a cock up.'

But Mrs Beaumont seemed oblivious to the time. Unwilling to spoil the pleasure of her outing, Kath maintained her composure as she rolled the wheelchair into the shop. The store was everything Kath had promised it would be. And although at one point she caught Mrs Beaumont's foot in a display stand, nearly sending it over, once they got to the perfume counter she began to relax. She knew there was enough room to park the wheelchair and allow Mrs Beaumont as much time as she needed to linger over all the perfumes while she stood back to consider her getting-home options.

But it was not to be. Although there were dozens of perfume samples on a counter tray, the counter itself was too high for Mrs Beaumont to reach from her chair. Thinking that the assistant would step in, and not wanting to interfere in Mrs Beaumont's decision, Kath retreated to the background. But the assistant, apparently blind to the difference between a rich old Chelsea lady and poor antipodean servant, ignored Mrs Beaumont and dealt directly with Kath.

'Mrs Beaumont doesn't get out often,' said Kath, hoping vainly that the assistant would take the hint. 'It's been a long time since she bought perfume and isn't familiar with all the new ones. Could she please try as many as possible?'

'What perfume does she use now?'

It was as if Mrs Beaumont were not there.

Kath had hoped they would encounter a pleasant and alert assistant capable of quickly summing up the situation and making the simple outing a special occasion for Mrs Beaumont. But it didn't work that way. Getting impatient, and aware of how little time they had, Kath had to intervene. Ordering the assistant about as if she, not Mrs Beaumont, were the wealthy customer, Kath organised samples of three or four of the best-known brands. From these samples Mrs Beaumont happily chose one and was delighted with her purchase. Chuckling with pleasure she clutched the little parcel to herself and off they went again, homeward bound.

Now, though, Mrs Beaumont noticed the time and was mildly concerned. Kath knew that she was mostly worried about Mr

Beaumont's angry reaction to her late return. Kath's only response was to reassure her by assuming an air of confidence. But she had a plan. She decided to watch out for a taxi; one with the wheelchair emblem signifying a taxi equipped with wheelchair ramps, wheel locks on the floor, and a driver trained to manage wheelchairs. She even decided that she would pay for the taxi herself so Mrs Beaumont wouldn't have to worry about the extravagance. But before she could find an appropriate taxi Mrs Beaumont spotted a flower and plant barrow parked in an alley. She insisted that Kath should make a detour to buy some pots of pansies.

This, Kath decided, was the last straw.

'I think we're running so late now we'd better get a taxi.'

'Oh, no, dear,' said Mrs Beaumont. She was evidently enjoying her outing now regardless of the consequences. 'We'll be all right. I know a shortcut from here.'

A shortcut. Apparently, if Kath followed her directions, and went really fast, they would be home fifteen minutes.

Fifteen minutes?

'I don't mind how fast you go, dear.'

So off they went. Up the side of the alley, and through streets and lanes that were new to Kath, until they found themselves at the back of the Royal Marsden Hospital. On they went, past loading bays, the boiler room, the laundry, the morgue. And all the time Mrs Beaumont was shouting directions, and pointing the way, while the plastic bag of pansy pots banged against the frame of the wheelchair.

Suddenly they were on the grass, a decorative lawn, forbidden, in full view of anyone looking out a window. Then through a shrubbery and around a corner. And there, at last, a wrought iron gate opening to the street.

But which street? Where? Kath had no idea. She stopped. Puzzled.

'This way,' shouted Mrs Beaumont, pointing, and Kath obeyed.

Suddenly they were on the familiar Fulham Road. At last. And only a block or two from the home turn.

'Now you know where you are, dear,' said Mrs Beaumont, relaxing in her chair. 'I'll leave the rest to you. But you can go a bit faster if you wish. I can hang on.'

Abandoning all caution, Kath ran. Fast. She was familiar enough with the road now to know where best to cross, which curbs to avoid, how to ensure that she didn't tip Mrs Beaumont out onto her face. And Mrs Beaumont, invigorated by the adventure, hung on to the wheelchair's arms for the final sprint home.

By the time they got home, at a quarter-to-one, Kath was exhausted. But Mrs Beaumont was fine and a few minutes later shuffled into the living room as if nothing had happened.

Kath knew better though. She knew that Mrs Beaumont enjoyed the excitement of the morning, was delighted with her perfume purchase, and her pansies, and was happy to be only fifteen minutes late. But Mr Beaumont was less than pleased. Despite his personal reluctance to venture out of the house he was jealous of his wife's independence. But now, relieved that she was home at last, glad that normality had been restored, he calmed down and fussed about at the bar with the usual routine.

'Would you like a Madeira, my dear? Or a sherry?'

She never wanted Madeira. Always sherry. But he never gave up asking.

'I think a sherry today, darling,' she replied, every day, sweetly and patiently.

Then they sat together sipping at the heavily fortified drinks, ordered especially from their agent in Bristol, that would put them both to sleep for the afternoon. They were waiting for lunch which they knew would emerge, at precisely one o'clock, from the kitchen below.

Later that day Mrs Beaumont had even more excitement when she received a visit from Lucie, a favourite granddaughter. Lucie was an especially bright, vivacious young woman who enjoyed her grandmother's company and paid regular visits. On this occasion she had come to say good-bye; she was off on a journey to India.

Before she left the house, though, Lucie came downstairs to say good-bye to us. She had a gift in her hand and was bubbling over with excitement.

'Look what gran gave me for a present,' she said. 'Isn't she lovely.'

And she showed us the bottle of perfume that her grandmother had purchased in the King's Road only that morning.

Chapter XV

'A LIGHT LUNCHEON AT ONE,' CELIA HAD SAID.

Into an old and cracked wooden bowl I put two lettuce leaves, four slices of peeled tomato — it had to be peeled — and four slices of peeled cucumber. This was the luncheon salad. It was exactly the same every day. Nothing but the old wooden bowl could be used and absolutely nothing else, including dressing of any sort, was permitted.

The salad was followed by the cheese board. A selection of crackers was kept in the dining room cabinet upstairs but the cheeses were kept in the kitchen refrigerator and needed replenishing and rearranging each day. Because of the otherwise unvarying routine I did my best to choose interesting cheeses — remarkably, I had some freedom in this respect — and arrange them on the board as attractively as I could. Then, hoping for a gastronomic breakthrough, I created decorative garnishes with colourful touches of radish, capsicum, celery, carrot, or something else similarly 'exotic' chosen from our own supplies.

At first I was encouraged to see that the little garnishes were missing when the cheeseboard was returned after lunch; perhaps, I thought, they are sampling the potential delights of a more varied salad.

But I was wrong. The French doors from the dining room were directly above the kitchen window and one day I was dismayed to see my little curls of cucumber skin, through which I had painstakingly laced *julienne* carrot or some other such thing, come sailing down from above and into the sunken courtyard beside the poor bay tree.

'The old bastard.'

We — Kath, Mariana and I — were enjoying our own lunch at the table in front of the kitchen window.

'Always he is doing it,' said Mariana.

'You knew?'

'I know it,' she said with a shrug. 'You waste your time with nice thingis, Bop. Mr Beaumont no like it.'

I watched the pigeons drop automatically from the roof to investigate these scraps but even they showed no interest in my handiwork.

'I bet Mrs Beaumont likes it though.'

'She no say nothing,' Mariana said.

'Well, bugger him.'

'No mind it,' Mariana said. 'Always he is the same. Many yearis.'

But it *didn't* stop me. Instead I purposely garnished the cheeseboard even more elaborately and it soon became a game to see how prettily I could decorate the cheeseboard and how long it took before my little embellishment was fired out the window. It was only a little thing, literally, but it made the three of us laugh every day.

After the salad and cheese Mr and Mrs Beaumont moved across to the comfort of the living room where Kath had served the coffee. How they managed to enjoy their coffee escaped me entirely. To begin with I was annoyed that it had to be served, as it always had been served, in a tall silver teapot. I tried to make the point that a matching and real coffee-pot — with the spout at the top where it belongs — was mouldering away in storage, below stairs, but without success. The teapot had to serve as the coffee-pot, and that was that. And that meant that some of the sludgy coffee grounds, which, unlike tea leaves, always sink to the bottom of the pot, were delivered into every cupful.

Furthermore I found that the mandatory method of brewing the coffee was appalling. But it had always been done the same way and, according to Celia at our briefing, reinforced daily by Mariana, there was no room for variation.

A special saucepan was assigned for the boiling of the water. Once the water was rolling — the worst condition for coffee water — the coffee grounds were tossed in and stirred vigorously. The mixture had to then sit — the exact sitting time was not specified — before being strained off into the alleged coffee-pot.

As a coffee lover I couldn't bear the destruction of the coffee's oils and essences in this way, let alone having to serve a beverage so muddy. I tried drinking it only once and was puzzled how they could drink it twice a day; it was thick and bitter. Its method of brewing, its burnt flavour, and its complete lack of aroma, all reminded me of making and drinking coffee around a campfire in the wild west. But this was west London not the wild west.

Special sugar crystals were purchased for the coffee to be used for nothing else. And from the thick syrupy dregs in the bottom of each empty cup I guessed that they used this expensive sugary sweetness to mask the horrible taste of the coffee.

But worse was to come: what was left of the coffee — in both the saucepan and the returned teapot/coffee-pot — had to be saved in a jug for reheating and serving again. While I persisted with the entrenched method of coffee brewing — without a coffee-maker I had no choice — I refused to reheat cold coffee; especially *that* cold coffee.

Out it went.

'What a waste,' said Kath sarcastically, wagging her finger at me. 'Celia will get you and you'll be in trouble.'

But Mariana was more serious.

'Is not good to waste it the coffee,' she said, catching me pouring the muddy mixture away. 'Celia will be angry.'

'She won't know.'

'She will find out it.' Her brow was creased with genuine worry as she watched the brown and gritty stuff disappear down the plug hole. 'She always knows it.'

Eventually I prevailed on Mrs Beaumont to let me buy an inexpensive plunger coffee-maker. She was sitting at the desk in her study before her walk. I loved to go into her study; it was full of photos and personal memorabilia, on walls and shelves, from her younger days before The Little Boltons, and I longed to be able to spend time in there on my own.

'How much will it cost?'

She was looking up at me from her chair and caught me eyeing her old photographs. She smiled faintly. Her hand was in the drawer where she kept the housekeeping money. I wish I could have ask her about her past.

'Pardon,' I said, embarrassed by my own curiosity.

'How much will it cost, Bob? The coffee-maker?'

I had done my research.

'Oh. About ten pounds I think.'

She gave me the money with a 'keep-cook-happy' look, unconvinced that the coffee would be any different or better, and said something pleasant and cheerful as she always did. Perhaps she referred to something Kath and she had discussed: 'So you enjoyed the ballet. Covent Garden is delightful. I used to go there so often you know.' Or she might say: 'Supper was very nice last night.' Or: 'That new cake was lovely, Bob. Splendid.'

Whether she was genuine, making polite small talk or trying to put me at ease I didn't know, but she had no idea how pleased I was with such simple compliments. I felt like a child, anxious to please a parent, and excited when my efforts were recognised.

I made a special bus trip — again to Peter Jones in Sloane Square but this time with cash in my pocket — to buy that coffee-maker. It was a minor triumph at the time although I don't think the old pair noticed any difference or improvement. Certainly no comment was made although, given the amount of the sugar they used, any change in the coffee flavour was probably beyond detection.

I realised then that they rarely did anything routine — such as drinking coffee — because they enjoyed it; rather they seemed to do it because, in their minds, it was somehow appropriate. It was as if they felt on show, anxious to do the *right* thing. Perhaps they had a mental picture of how they wanted to appear to the world; a picture based not on how other people of their class lived but how they *imagined* they lived, or how they imagined they had lived in years gone by.

It was a distorted picture, blurred by time and enlarged by imagination. And yet there was no-one of their generation left to impress. Only their own busy and preoccupied families, Mariana, and us.

Chapter XVI

APART FROM THE RELIGIOUS LOCKING AND UN-locking of the house, and an outing to town every Thursday, feeding the local pigeons was Mr Beaumont's only self-imposed and regular duty. However, the original purpose of this chore seemed to have been forgotten; the feeders he used were actually squirrel feeders, and the peanuts he filled them with more appropriate to those little creatures, especially in the winter. But although the timid squirrels had surrendered their feeders to the aggressive and more numerous pigeons, who incidentally created thick little hillocks of guano below each feeder, Mr Beaumont kept up the feeding ritual without question.

He had fixed the wire feeders to the back of the house in two convenient — convenient for him — locations. One was set at stretching height above the upstairs garden door which led onto the patio and thence down to the garden, the other at a similar height above the downstairs garden door. Whenever he noticed that these bent and rusty contrivances were empty he refilled them from a large sack of shelled peanuts which stood in the laundry beside the large barrel of salt used to soften the heating water.

'S'like a bleedin' salted peanuts factory in 'ere,' said Fergus the handyman.

Every couple of days, usually in the morning while Mrs Beaumont was out on her walk and I was working in the kitchen, I heard the electric chair coming downstairs. Then I recognised the sound of his shuffling to the laundry where he slowly but methodically refilled each feeder, littering the floor with peanuts in the process. Sometimes, during the refilling process, I wandered into the laundry to see how he was managing but my presence seemed to unsettle him.

As if embarrassed by his own charity he debased it with his own words.

'Damn birds,' he always said. 'Dashed nuisance. Don't know why I bother. Can't stretch up as I used to.'

Thinking that perhaps he was seeking volunteers I offered to help.

'Look here,' he said quickly with an edge of resentment in his voice. He was stooping over the big peanut bag, an orange plastic scoop in his hand. His head was pushed forward and hanging low, like a threatened animal, and his eyes were peering at me over the top of his spectacles. He stared, almost angrily; a look that meant that once again he felt threatened. But by what I knew not.

Then, just as quickly, he relaxed. Stood up.

'My job,' he said at last. 'Been doing it for years. Can't think why. All these nut things. Have to get rid of them.'

When each feeder was eventually restored to its outside position he retired to the dining room to stand and watch the birds fall to them from their roosts on the roof.

The constant presence of the fat overfed pigeons, greedily feeding and fighting above each of the back doors, had an unfortunate but inevitable side-effect which collected in white hillocks at each doorstep. While it was interesting that the old man should spend money, time and not inconsiderable effort on feeding these unpleasant creatures, and peculiar that he should choose to do so while most of London was trying to eliminate them as no better than flying rats, I found the presence of their little white hills of guano to be especially disgusting. And I wasn't the only one.

In the summer Mrs Beaumont liked to go into the garden. As it was necessary for Kath to help her, and as she inevitably went very slowly out the door, it was impossible for her to miss the white pigeon mess as she shuffled across the doorstep.

'Do you think Bob would clean this up, dear?' she asked every time.

But I refused. I hated that stuff and considered the act of scrubbing the concrete steps clean of bird droppings to be entirely inappropriate for someone handling old people's food.

'They're too old,' I protested. 'One little microbe of bird-borne disease and they'd have no chance. It's too risky.'

Much to my discomfort and shame I allowed Kath to collect the necessary hot and disinfected water and scrubbing brush, and kneel on the landing to scrape and scrub away the offending material. On particularly hot, dry days, when it was especially hard to dispose of even the remaining blemish on the concrete, I condescended to help by rinsing away the residue with a high-pressure hose. It was one of the most unpleasant of our duties, and the one that caused the most friction between us.

Mr Beaumont was inordinately proud of his house in The Little Boltons but seemed to have forgotten that even the most valuable and well-built house requires constant maintenance. His was in fact an old house — built about eighteen-sixty — and was looking tired and in need of a spruce up. He didn't seem to notice its increasingly shabby appearance, which was unfortunate but didn't affect the building's integrity, but I knew there were structural problems which really *did* matter and would have to be attended to before long.

But drawing attention to defects in his house — even with the best of intentions — was interpreted by Mr Beaumont as a personal insult. The house, his home for more than fifty years, had become an extension of his person and he guarded it from criticism as if he were protecting his own body.

Our bathroom, across the top landing and opposite our bedroom, was a real problem. The white-tiled room was pleasant enough despite the flaking paint and unshaded light. It was furnished with a heavy cast-iron bath, and a bulky vitreous-china basin and toilet of the post-war vintage now sought-after by collectors and museums. But there was no shower. At first we made-do with the bath but apart from being unaccustomed to sitting in our own dirty water the bath's enamel surface was badly pitted and exceedingly uncomfortable to sit on. It was out of the question to have a shower installed so we bought a flexible shower hose with adjustable fittings that could be fixed to the existing taps.

It worked adequately, at least we could shower again, but it was not long enough for us to stand under. And as there was no way to fix it to the wall anyway we still had to sit in the bottom of the pitted, scratchy bath, holding the shower hose with one hand and trying to wash with the other.

Apart from this inconvenience, to which we never became accustomed, the bathroom door frequently swung open on its own. It did so because the bathroom floor — perhaps the entire top floor — had moved; it now sloped so much that the bathroom door frame was misaligned and the door latch no longer reached deeply enough into the door jamb. Clearly a load-bearing floor joist had given way below, with dry rot or something, and would soon demand major reconstruction.

I knew that Mr Beaumont couldn't, wouldn't and didn't come up to our floor and so wouldn't know about the problem of the collapsing floor. Thinking I was doing the right thing I mentioned it to him one day when he was in the kitchen.

'Nothing wrong with the floor,' he said angrily. 'Stuff and nonsense.'

I personally didn't think the floor falling in was 'stuff and nonsense' but I dropped the subject then but mentioned it later to Mrs Beaumont's son Julian. He also, but for different reasons, didn't want to know.

'I'd forget about it if I were you, old man,' he said. 'He just doesn't like to know about these things so I'm not going to tell him. Are you?'

'I already have.'

Julian grimaced, tightening the sinews in his neck.

'Oh dear,' he said bravely. 'Jolly shame. Never mind. We'll muddle through I suppose.'

But it was we who had to muddle through. The subject was never raised again and nothing was ever done about the sloping bathroom floor and the door that swung open at the most inconvenient and inappropriate moments. Fortunately it was our bathroom on our floor to which nobody ever came to breach our privacy.

That Mr Beaumont did take my advice once took me completely by surprise. Knowing Celia was always concerned about his appearance I often tried to act like a valet. Usually my attempts to help were rebuffed but once, when I suggested he needed a haircut, he agreed although I didn't know about it until later.

'Fabio is going to take Mr Beaumont for a drive in the car today,' Mariana announced the next morning. 'Mrs Beaumont has agreed it. Will be good for Mr Beaumont, yes?'

'When?' I asked.

'This afternoon. When Mrs Beaumont is rest. I am going to go home, and after it me and Fabio will come with the car. Fabio is going to get Mr Beaumont a haircut.'

It was a special outing and, surprisingly, Mr Beaumont was looking forward to it. After lunch he fetched his hat and coat, laid them on the back of the couch in readiness, and waited. Fabio and Mariana arrived in their old Mercedes and parked it in the drive. I let them in the front door. Mariana was dressed up a little, at least she wasn't wearing her housekeeping clothes, but Fabio seemed to have made a special effort; or perhaps he had come straight from work. He was dressed in a black suit with a bright white shirt and a black tie: he looked suave and handsome. His silver hair was thick and wavy, his face was dark, and his smile was white, wide and sincere.

'How are you, Bop?' he said with a wink, shaking my right hand with one hand and squeezing my right shoulder hard with the other.

Mariana was excited and proud.

'Mr Beaumont,' she said, in the living room. 'Fabio is here. We go for a driving now. Okay?'

Out of her housekeeping role she was a different person and treated Mr Beaumont with the sort of gentleness and respect kind people reserve for the very old or the very young. There was not the slightest trace of the nervousness or servility frequently evident during the working part of her day.

Mr Beaumont stood up when they came in and greeted Fabio like an old friend. They remained standing in the living room for some time, talking and laughing. Mr Beaumont looked remarkably relaxed and cheerful. He talked freely, threw his head back with laughter, and patted Fabio on the back with genuine manly affection. But Fabio looked less relaxed. He appeared to be perplexed by Mr Beaumont's unexpected familiarity. It was so unusual that I wondered, seriously but unfairly, if Mr Beaumont actually knew who Fabio was.

Then they were ready to leave. Fabio helped Mr Beaumont into his coat, handed him his hat, and followed as Mariana led them out of the room. While Mariana got into the front of the car Fabio helped Mr Beaumont get into the back. When the old man was quite settled and comfortable Fabio closed the door in much the same way I supposed that he did at his hotel. Then he came around to the back of the car and stood with me while he finished his cigarette.

'Is good peoples, Bop,' he said. 'But Mr Beaumont is going out not enough. Mariana said it. Is true. They enjoy the car. I go.' He stepped on his cigarette — I'll have to sweep up that later, I thought — pointed his finger at me, winked and said: 'Hey, Bop. He goes. You the boss now, eh.'

When they returned, and they were not gone long, Mr Beaumont's white hair was well shortened, especially at the back where it tended to get wispy and shaggy over his collar.

'Dashed peculiar,' Kath overheard him say to his wife. 'Woman. Cut my hair. Never seen anything like it. Women everywhere. Dickens of a place.'

'Where did you go?' I asked Mariana the next morning.

'King's Road. Is where I was going. Is good and cheap. Ten poundis is all.'

Is all? That was three times what I would pay at home. But I knew the place and had been there myself on Mariana's recommendation. A plain little shop in an unfashionable part of that famous road, it bustled with young, trendy, transient, female hairdressers with tight jeans and beaded hair, rocking to a high-volume FM radio station. It was a good place, a friendly place, and it was relatively cheap. But I doubted whether Mr Beaumont had ever been anywhere like it in his life.

Chapter XVII

ALTHOUGH OUR HOURS WERE LONG, DICTATED BY the rising and retiring of our employers, and getting time off was never easy, we did have the luxury of a short rest period most afternoons. It came because after lunch each day Mrs Beaumont took an afternoon nap. It was Mariana who helped her to bed at this time, her last duty before she went home, and as it was the only time she was alone with Mrs Beaumont she took the opportunity to discuss her work, her wages and her holidays.

While she was doing that Kath and I cleaned up after lunch. In the living room upstairs Mr Beaumont settled into his armchair for the afternoon. There, with heavy old head resting in a propped-up hand, he dozed the afternoon away in warm, comfortable, oblivious bliss.

There were never callers to the house in the afternoon — it was as if the whole of London was resting — and for the first time all day the house was peaceful and quiet. From then until it was time to prepare tea, and providing one of us remained in the house in case of an emergency, we were free to do whatever we wished. Often all we wanted to do was rest, even sleep.

While I was usually able to listen to the radio as I worked in the kitchen, the afternoon was the first chance either of us had to read. The papers, by now crumpled and disordered, were cleared from the living room after lunch and we took them all to our top floor room where we could straighten them out and read them at leisure. This was also the time for reading letters, and writing them, or for planning our weekend day-and-a-bit off. It was a genuinely restful, recreational period which succeeded in restoring us for the long hours ahead. Indeed, never did two workers — whose working hours stretched from seven o'clock in the morning until nine or ten at night — so appreciate their little break in the day.

This was the time, too, when I most appreciated our high position looking out over the garden, and those adjacent, to The Boltons beyond. Although at ground level the garden walls were high, they appeared insignificant from our great height. By ignoring them it was easy to imagine being in the country, looking across and through a lightly wooded coppice to a street of houses in a sleepy but prosperous village. The effect was heightened by the sharp needle of Saint Mary The Boltons which pierced the leafiness of the tall horse chestnuts; on hot still days it looked like a pretty picture of Nutwood from a Rupert Bear book.

But it was an illusion. I knew that the strip of land running between The Boltons and The Little Boltons all the way to Old Brompton Road and Bolton Gardens, was not really an idyllic coppice, a wildlife retreat, but was severely divided into neat rectangles, laid out more than a hundred years since, marked by stone walls taller than a tall man.

Whether the Victorian planners and builders knew it or not — and perhaps they did — these walls, which I could hardly see from high, had turned this relatively open part of inner London into a wildlife desert. Because although the tall trees and neat gardens softened the urban edge, the walls restricted the natural range of small animals and, instead, created cruel cages in which they simply couldn't survive.

Looking down on our garden, from our lofty vantage point in the roof, I was enchanted to know that Beatrix Potter's garden, too, must have once looked as this one did. She used to live in a house nearby, in Bolton Gardens on Old Brompton Road; it and its neighbours were bombed to rubble during the war and a primary school was built in their place. Only a simple plaque on the school wall, set off by coloured reliefs of Peter Rabbit and Jemima Puddleduck, remained to mark the place that was once the Potter home.

I was puzzled by Beatrix Potter's intimate knowledge of small animals, such as rabbits and hedgehogs, as I had seen none in our garden, and knew there could have been none in hers, but I found the answer after only a little library research. And in the process I wondered why a library located almost directly opposite the place where one of the English language's most beloved writers had lived for so long showed no particular interest in her or her life.

Was there a library on the site at the time? Was the young Miss Potter a member? Indeed, should it now be called The Beatrix Potter Memorial Library? But it was a library like any other, with no more or less material on Beatrix Potter than one would expect.

From my reading there I learned that even in her childhood the neighbourhood could support few wild animals. Only the birds and squirrels, to whom walls mean nothing, and the insects, whose range is so small, survived as remnants of the area's rural past. From a young age, however, Beatrix was a constant visitor to the countryside and it was partly in this way — and through her frequent visits to the nearby Natural History Museum — that the girl and young woman acquired her intimate knowledge of the personality, behaviour and appearance of England's wild and farmyard creatures.

That she managed to distil this knowledge into a series of little coloured illustrations, in which my favourite, Mrs Tiggy-winkle, always looks exactly as a hedgehog should, even in the cap and apron of a washerwoman, remains an artistic wonder. And that she was able to translate the fussy, particular nature of a hedgehog — carefully washing, clear-starching, ironing and airing all her neighbours' clothes — into her text remains one of her greatest charms.

It was during one of her country holidays in the north that Beatrix abducted her Mrs Tiggy-winkle and brought her back to her home in Bolton Gardens. But because the garden was so small, perhaps only one quarter or less of what a hedgehog would need to survive naturally, she had to care for Mrs Tiggy-winkle by hand. But even under the tender care of a sensitive, recluse woman, the short-lived hedgehog grew old and infirm.

'I am sorry to say that I am upset about poor Tiggy,' Beatrix wrote to a friend in August, nineteen-hundred-and-five. 'She hasn't seemed well the last fortnight and has begun to be sick, and she is so thin. I am afraid that the long course of unnatural diet and indoor life is beginning to tell on her. It is a wonder she has lasted so long. I hope she will either get well or go quickly.'

But Tiggy didn't get well, nor 'go quickly', and before long, much to Beatrix's distress, her dear little friend became desperately ill. So

Beatrix Potter, now thirty-nine years old and still grieving over the recent death of her beloved *fiancé,* acquired some chloroform and put the prickly little lady to sleep. When she was sure all life had left the creature she excavated a small grave in her back garden, under one of the chestnut trees, and laid her pet to rest.

The book was very descriptive of the family home at number two Bolton Gardens and of the back garden trees under one of which was laid the dead Mrs Tiggy-winkle. There were even photographs of the trellis-topped garden wall and a line of trees that looked especially familiar.

Thus, for some afternoons, while the rest of the house slept, I spent my time in the library. One afternoon, library book in hand, I walked across Old Brompton Road and wandered up South Bolton Gardens, a short street off The Little Boltons which once marked the back boundary of the Potter house. The houses in the first half of the street were still standing and were similar in size and style to the Potter house, and it was easy to recognise their back garden wall as being the same style of bricklaying and trellis as that shown in the Potter photograph. Obviously this same wall once ran the entire length of the street's back gardens.

Following the line of the wall led me to the gate of Bousfield Primary School which took up the space of the houses numbers one to six, thus including the Potter house. With no-one about during class hours I nervously sneaked into the school playground.

Soon, I knew, many children would come running out of class and across this playground, as thousands must have run across it before, into the care of the mothers, fathers and nannies who were already beginning to assemble at the gate. Few of them, if any — adults or children — could know what took place here on that sad day so long ago. But I did, and I was glad. And it seemed appropriate to me that what was once Beatrix Potter's back garden was now a school playground.

I stood there on my own, quietly contemplating the writer's sad, oppressed childhood; a strict Victorian childhood in which a domineering father forced her to remain at home. An awful, lonely life without which she never would have had the time to so closely observe God's creatures and create the little books which, ironically, have brought so much childhood joy to so many of the generations that followed her.

Then, with open book in hand, and moist eyes casting down to the photograph and then up to the playground, I was easily able to identify the very line of trees that once stood at the bottom of the Potter garden. Larger now, with more green wood at their base and each surrounded by a low, stone wall, it was nevertheless possible to recognise the angle of each bole and the shape and pattern of the branching. But it was all an open space now, paved as a playground without garden walls, with the trees forming a natural avenue leading to the school buildings. And although I didn't know exactly which was the important tree, I knew that beneath one of them, under the asphalt over which children had run and played for some forty years, lay the tiny bones of dear Mrs Tiggy-winkle.

Walking home, preparing myself for the usual tea and supper rush, and hoping that nothing had happened to the Beaumonts in my absence, I couldn't get Beatrix Potter off my mind. One day, I knew, we would have to leave The Little Boltons and the thought made me sad. These houses. These streets. These gardens. These walls. They were familiar to me already and they must have been even more familiar to her. Because this, I knew, was where she had lived for forty-seven years. And the fact that Mrs Tiggy-winkle's little grave remained unmarked and forgotten made me especially sad.

Surely, I thought, Beatrix Potter and Mrs Tiggy-winkle deserved more than a plaque on the outside of a school wall. Surely this place, this little school, could dedicate something more fitting to the history of the site and to the poignant memory of that little event which happened, in its own playground, not so very long ago.

Chapter XVIII

THURSDAY AFTERNOONS WERE MORE PEACEFUL than most because Mr Beaumont was out of the house almost the entire day.

He began his Thursdays as usual. When he got up he selected clean underwear, a clean shirt and the suit he wore only on Thursdays. He followed his morning routine rigidly — unlocking the front door, collecting the newspapers, drawing back the living room drapes and folding away the shutters, unlocking all the internal doors and switching off the gate light — and the breakfast service was the same as usual.

But after breakfast it all changed. A taxi was ordered; he donned his hat and overcoat and stood in the living room, waiting. With Celia's instructions in mind I tried to act like a valet and surprisingly he let me help him. It was in fact one of the rare times I was allowed upstairs. I met him in the hall to turn down his collar, straighten his tie and brush him down. He seemed to enjoy this treatment and the fact that I saw him to his taxi and stood at the door until he had gone.

But quite where he went on those all-important Thursdays, and exactly what he did, I didn't know. I did know that his first stop was his bank — Coutts & Co. in Old Park Lane — where, presumably, he saw to whatever of his affairs needed his attention, cashing a cheque for Mrs Beaumont that went towards both the house's food and Kath's wages.

For some reason Mr and Mrs Beaumont not only shared the cost of our wages equally but also treated us separately; it was at their Friday morning meeting, the day after Mr Beaumont's trip to town, that Mrs Beaumont handed Kath her wages of one-hundred-and-fifty pounds cash in an envelope while I received a personal cheque for the same amount from her husband. It suited us well: we spent the cash and banked the cheque and, with few expenses, our savings quickly grew.

Where the taxi waited in the busy streets of Mayfair, while Mr Beaumont was in the bank, I didn't know. But it must have waited, somewhere, until he returned. Then it carried him and his full wallet to one of his clubs in Piccadilly where he first had lunch and then spent a good part of the afternoon enjoying more than a few gins. It was always late in the day when he arrived home, again by taxi, tiddly, aggressive and argumentative.

'Just ignore him,' was Julian's advice. 'He's a typical bully. Just don't take any notice of him. I don't.'

Julian was right, of course: he *was* a typical bully who preferred to insult women rather than men. Full of bluff and bluster, and lacking a quick wit, he avoided proper verbal contests resorting instead to an overworked collection of well-rehearsed slurs that were clumsily barbed and poorly directed. But they could still hurt the weak and vulnerable.

It was this propensity for end-of-the-day argument that spoiled our otherwise peaceful Thursdays. We knew from experience how rude he could be on any day, and how much more rude he could be on Thursdays. Mostly we avoided being his target. But eventually, one Thursday evening, his grumpiness fuelled by too many gins, he reduced Kath to tears while she was serving supper. It was such a pity because that particular Thursday — a royal day — was one which she had been looking forward to for so long.

We were free of household duties that Thursday simply because Mrs Beaumont couldn't refuse Kath's request for time off to attend a royal event especially as Mr Beaumont was to be out of the house all day and Mariana had agreed to stay with Mrs Beaumont until we returned.

'Ascot? The Queen? Of course, you must go, dear. Both of you,' she said. 'But I've never heard of such a thing. How did you manage it?'

'Oh, I just wrote away asking for a ticket,' said Kath vaguely, her nonchalance concealing her excitement, her year-long letter-writing campaign now forgotten.

But it was not 'Ascot' Ascot for which we had a ticket; it was for an associated royal occasion which, in Kath's opinion at least, was better than Ascot. An occasion which meant, she said, we would get very close to the royals, closer than anyone at Ascot.

Kath had discovered that each day of Royal Ascot whichever members of the royal family were attending the course were driven, in a cavalcade of cars, from the back of Windsor Castle, down the Long Walk and through the winding lanes of the Great Park, which was otherwise closed for the day, to where their horse-drawn carriages were waiting. There, without ceremony, they all piled out of their modern limousines — they were called 'motors' on the official carriage list — and into their ridiculously old-fashioned horse-carriages for the short ride to Ascot where they made a formal, royal and very horsey entrance.

By applying properly, and in time, Kath had obtained one of the few tickets for entry to the Great Park where members of the public waited at the edge of the lane to view the transfer from limousines to carriages. Entry tickets were issued for cars only with no apparent limit to the number of people in each car. Our niece Lisa was happy to provide the car in return for entrance rights to this little-known event and a share of our picnic.

'Vehicles must leave the park immediately the Royal Procession has passed' said the large green ticket we had been instructed to display in the car's front window. Thus we had purposely left London early because we wanted to have our picnic first and then spend as much time in the park as possible before the royal procession.

Once inside Ascot Gate it was easy to find somewhere to park. The empty carriages were waiting in line, under an avenue of trees, and so we unloaded our rugs and our picnic hamper and established ourselves on the grass verge beside them. We had our picnic lunch there and were then free to wander about the immediate vicinity and approach the waiting procession line as closely as we wished. It was remarkably easy and informal; an altogether low-key affair.

The waiting carriages — all open — were mostly shiny black and of relatively modern lines; they looked especially sleek and graceful in the park environment. Their horses stood patiently in harness; some drooped their heads while others looked around listlessly, stamping their feet sharply with boredom. Occasionally a whinny or a blow broke through the ambient human chatter, and the shaking of a heavy head caused polished tack to rattle and clink. Meanwhile the red-and-gold suited riders, anxious for the welfare of their mounts, leaned forward in their tiny saddles to adjust straps, bridles and reins — patting and rubbing thick, well-groomed necks in the process — while their similarly-suited colleagues on the ground fussed about, checking the security of shafts and the tightness of girth straps.

Then, suddenly, in response to some silent signal, the men tensed as one and, making final adjustments to their helmets and top hats, took their places on horseback, driving seat or beside carriage door, where they remained, looking forward with rigidly held heads, until the cars arrived.

Now, looking back through the trees towards the castle, which was literally miles away and thus well out of sight, I saw a line of long black cars, speeding — yes, speeding — through the park towards us, glinting in the sun and throwing sharp, sparkling needles of light though the trees. In what seemed only a few seconds they slowed, rounded the last corner, and glided towards us in complete silence, coming to a stop in a line to the right of the waiting carriages.

Because both cars and carriages were arranged in the same processional order, when the Queen's car stopped at the front carriage each following car was automatically placed adjacent to its appropriate carriage. And because the assorted royals had each managed to get into their assigned car in the correct order, the transfer of people from the left-side doors of the cars to the right-side doors of the carriages was executed smoothly, swiftly, and largely out of sight.

That so many people could move from one line of vehicles to another so quickly, without speaking, without confusion, impressed me immensely. My own family couldn't do it without getting out of line, shouting and arguing, falling over, dropping something or leaving something behind. But the royal family did it smoothly that day; I supposed they were well used to it.

Once everyone was settled, and at another coded signal from someone, the horses were touched, and I watched, impressed, as they leaned forward into their collars and with a single effortless pull broke the inertia of their wheeled burdens and rolled them off elegantly to Royal Ascot.

As the least interested of our small party in the royal goings-on I had been assigned to photographic duty. So while Kath and Lisa stood as close as they could to see as much as they could I assumed a roving portfolio, moving up and down the line to capture both the wider picture and as many close-ups as I could. Unfortunately, though, it was a case of too much of a good thing: faced with so many royals at once, so many carriages and horses, so much pageantry in such a small space, so many photo ops at the same time, I became confused and flustered, overwhelmed by over-choice, and, to Kath's disgust, got only one decent photograph from the whole day.

But my mental pictures are crystal clear: the immaculate presentation of cars, carriages, horses and uniforms; the military-like precision of the transfer process; and a closer view of the Queen in pink and grey, the Duke of Edinburgh and Prince Charles than I would have believed possible. We were all so close to each other that the Queen, her husband, son, sister and various cousins, nobles and staff, could look us in the eye, and we could look them in the eye, and the smiles on both sides were as sincere as I have seen on anyone. They passed, and I, feeling like a peasant in my jeans, t-shirt and baseball cap, with dangling camera, stood looking, amazed, at the receding procession as it bobbed and jogged away between the thin lines of happy, smiling, waving, jumping-with-joy people that lined each side of the path all the way to the park exit.

That Ascot Thursday evening, while Kath was serving dessert in the dining room and I was doing the dishes downstairs, I heard, through the hole in the ceiling, Mr Beaumont call Kath an 'incompetent, nincompoop colonial'. It was a sudden and appallingly rude outburst and I heard Kath gasp with shock and surprise.

Apparently she had placed a fork crookedly, or had delivered the wrong serving spoon, or had forgotten some petty detail of table protocol which Mr Beaumont considered essential to the proper enjoyment of his meal.

Forgetting all that I had learned, all that Julian had told me, that I was forbidden upstairs, and entirely heedless of the consequences, I dashed upstairs in my singlet, with a tea towel over my shoulder and wet pink rubber gloves on my hands. Without hesitation I opened the door of the dining room and entered without ceremony.

It was like a nineteenth-century stage farce: the innocent maid, Kath, standing to one side of the table, gripping the edge of her apron and holding it up to her open mouth, while I, the hero, threw open the door with a flourish and dashed onto the stage to rescue her from the dastardly villain.

'Mr Beaumont,' I said angrily, squeakily pulling off my still-wet and very pink rubber gloves as if ready to challenge him to a duel. 'You are a rude and inconsiderate old man.'

He was completely taken aback.

'I say, look here,' he said, standing up and throwing his napkin to the table. I waited, ready for an argument. (Or a duel?) 'Why the Dickens won't people pronounce my name properly?'

I was flabbergasted.

'What?' This was new. I had no idea what he was talking about.

'Dashed annoying,' he said, standing tall and straight with indignation.

It was so ridiculous that I laughed. And Kath, wiping her now moist eyes with her apron, laughed too. Mrs Beaumont, only half-hearing the encounter, looked up, dazed and bewildered, a serving spoon in her hand.

'What *are* you doing, Harold?' she asked, annoyed. 'Do sit down. We haven't had our pudding yet.'

He sat down, replaced his napkin, and ritually adjusted the silverware. Kath resumed the service. I left the room somewhat sheepishly. And the episode was never mentioned again.

Chapter XIX

WHILE MANY THINGS ABOUT A SERVANT'S LIFE IN the Royal Borough must have changed for the better since those far-off days Victorian and Edwardian days, we found that arranging time off in nineteen ninety-two was surely more difficult than it would have been a hundred or more years ago.

Conventions existed then concerning time off for servants which decent employers followed without question. And there were always other servants to fill in for those off duty. But those days were gone. We were the only live-in servants, we naturally wanted time off together, and the Beaumonts knew nothing of past conventions. It then became clear how important Prudence's advice was — that we should have a contract with absolutely everything in writing — when we had to give up any idea of having an evening off during the week.

Virtually a standard condition of employment in positions such as ours, an evening off was simply impossible at The Little Boltons. No member of the family would volunteer to cover for us during the week, and even if one were willing we would first have to make, serve and clean up the Beaumonts' supper, a routine that took until after nine o'clock most evenings; a little late to start an evening 'off'.

A contract seemed to be the only way we would ever get the night off we deserved — needed — once a week but it was too late. We lobbied the family and they were all sympathetic and supportive but nothing happened. I even drafted a contract myself but neither I nor any member of the family could get Mr and Mrs Beaumont to even consider it.

Were we being taken advantage of? Probably. Did we care? Not really. It was more a matter of principle. Realistically, an evening off was impossible to arrange.

We did manage to get agreement concerning weekends: we should have every Saturday afternoon off and all day Sunday, and every fourth weekend off entirely. It was also customary in the house, and therefore acceptable, that we should have off those public holidays which for some reason the British call bank holidays.

But nothing in this arrangement was as easy as it seemed. Even the agreed time off was granted only reluctantly by Mrs Beaumont — in fact we never had those fourth weekends off — and were left in no doubt that our desire to escape the house was selfish and that our absence was inconvenient in the extreme. It was true that Mr and Mrs Beaumont couldn't be left alone — they were probably *afraid* of being alone and simply couldn't manage without help — which meant a substitute had to be found every weekend. But it was always an *ad hoc* arrangement which always left us nervous and uncertain.

Mariana was our most obvious proxy. She understood the running of the house, and the Beaumonts' needs, even better than we did and certainly better than any family members. But she had her own life, her own home and family, and naturally her weekends off were as precious to her as ours were to us. And even though she best knew what was required, and even though I prepared all the meals in advance, it was still a lot of work for one person if the necessary standards were to be maintained.

And they *had* to be maintained.

Mariana also resented the way her employers could still make her feel guilty after twenty-five years.

'I don't want it to be here on Saturday nightis,' she said. 'But what can I do. The families is no good for it.'

She was referring to the duty roster — the English called it a rota — which the family members had drawn up to cover the times when we were off and Mariana wouldn't or couldn't fill in. Since I prepared all the meals in advance it was not much more than a roster of passive baby-sitting; just being there. But Mr and Mrs Beaumont didn't like it at all. It seemed wrong to them. They wanted their children to be guests not servants. But without us or

Mariana there to help they couldn't treat their children as guests, and they couldn't bring themselves to treat them as servants, so they had to reduce their demands and lower their standards. Thus they found the times when the family members were on duty to be unsettling and stressful.

Guilt again. When Mariana was our replacement we felt guilty for depriving her of her time at home; and if family-members were our replacements we felt guilty knowing how stressful it was for them all, Mr and Mrs Beaumont and the rostered family.

Making things feel as normal as possible in our absence, thus minimising Mr and Mrs Beaumont's stress, meant the pre-preparation of meals that were as near as possible the same as those served during the week. But that wasn't easy because I had to prepare things that would be easy and safe to reheat when reheating without a microwave oven — using the enormous, ancient and somewhat dangerous gas oven — was a daunting task for the uninitiated or nervous.

The potential menu had been made easier in a surprising and unexpected way. Kath had discovered from Mrs Beaumont that she and her husband liked *lasagne.* How they acquired a taste for this — for them — remarkably exotic dish we never discovered. Mrs Beaumont couldn't even pronounce it — she said something that sounded like 'ler-zarn' — and, given the English rule of one not eating what one couldn't pronounce, their enjoyment of *lasagne* was even more remarkable.

As Mrs Beaumont had long ago banned onions and garlic from the kitchen — an ancient ban which I simply ignored, much to Mariana's horror — I'm sure the dear and adamant lady didn't even know what was in 'ler-zarn'. In fact of all that dish's ingredients I'm sure she was familiar only with the minced meat, the salt and the pepper. But I used the banned onions and garlic, as I used oregano and parmesan cheese which I'm sure would also have been banned by Mrs Beaumont if only she had known of their existence.

Lasagne; I cannot now see it on a menu without calling it 'ler-zarn', and cannot enjoy it without reflecting upon the mystery of how two such aged and conservative English folk could themselves eat it without wondering whence came such strong, exotic and unfamiliar flavours and aromas.

But for all its strangeness *lasagne* was the ideal dish for preparing in advance and was enjoyed so much in our absence — by Mr and Mrs Beaumont and their family minders — that it became a regular feature of the weekend menu. If only they knew what was in it.

I made sure that soup — safe and easy to reheat and serve — was always available at the weekends by making more than necessary during the week and freezing what was left in convenient two-person servings. This, or a cold *entrée* such as smoked salmon or a favourite *pâté*, was quick and easy for Mariana or the family to prepare and serve.

I also prepared a cold dessert. Apple *strudel* was always a favourite and was ideal for serving cold; and any *parfait*, *mousse* or fruit 'fool' — a silly name for a simple cold fruit whip — especially served with their favourite and expensive cottage-made ice cream, kept them sated if not entirely happy in our absence. Thus, on Saturday nights at least, Mariana was able to maintain the three-course-meal regime on her own. And the serving of familiar-looking and -tasting dishes reassured Mr and Mrs Beaumont that everything was normal.

But our weekends were never really 'off'. Again and again we were the victims of that moral hold employers have over servants who live in their house. We may have been entitled to have the weekend off but in practice Mariana didn't arrive until eleven o'clock on Saturday morning which meant Kath still had to help Mrs Beaumont get up and get ready for the day, I had to prepare breakfast and Kath had to serve it and the coffee, and we had to clean up the kitchen afterwards. In other words, business as usual.

Mariana remained in the house for the day and slept the night, arranging lunch and tea, serving the supper which I had prepared in advance, cleaning up the dishes and the kitchen, and then waiting around, as Kath had to do each night, until Mrs Beaumont was ready for bed.

While we sometimes would have enjoyed having a quiet Saturday at home, especially in bad weather, we found it impossible to ignore what was happening or not happening in the rest of the house. The only way to escape the routine of the house was to go out for the afternoon and evening and leave Mariana to manage on her own.

But that presented another problem. Weekend or not Mr Beaumont always followed his locking-up routine. While Mariana helped Mrs Beaumont to bed in the evening he did the rounds of the house, closing the shutters, turning on the gate light and locking everything including the front door. The fact that we were out didn't matter; the door had to be locked, with its five locks, as it had been every night for fifty years.

In effect we were locked out every Saturday night.

Evidently this was not a new problem. Nor, I assumed, was it a problem confined to this house as I found the system devised by the family to overcome it mentioned in Forster's *Howards End* which was set about 1910. It was a simple system: a little tent-shaped cardboard sign had been fabricated on one side of which was printed the word 'IN' in thick blue letters and, on the other, 'OUT' in thick red letters. The idea was that if anyone — in this case we — should be out of the house at night the 'OUT' sign should be left on the table beside the front door to inform the compulsive locker-upper that a complete locking-up operation was not appropriate because someone was 'out'. If the 'out' person or persons returned before the locker-upper had retired they were to turn the 'OUT' sign to 'IN' to inform him that those who were 'out' were now 'in' and that he could safely complete the locking up process. If the 'out' person or persons returned after Mr Beaumont had retired then they were required to complete the locking up process on his behalf.

Apparently it was a system that had worked once but in our experience the little red sign was not enough to overcome Mr Beaumont's locking up habit of fifty years. Thus, red 'OUT' sign or not, the front door was locked and bolted every Saturday night before we got home. As if she didn't have enough to do Mariana had to stay awake until Mr Beaumont was asleep. Once she was confident that he was sleeping soundly she would creep downstairs to unlock and unbolt all the locks leaving only the single lock for which we had a key.

Once inside I had to lock all the locks and bolts, repeating the entire process which Mr Beaumont had so earnestly conducted only an hour or so since. It was an affair that was repeated every

Saturday night without exception and we laughed about it with Mariana every Sunday morning.

Sunday was our only real day off but even that was spoiled.

Mariana prepared and served Sunday morning's breakfast and then remained in the house until the assigned family member or members arrived for the afternoon and evening duty. We used those full Sundays to see as much as we could of London and England, setting off early, usually by train, and usually returning by about eight o'clock. Although we were still technically off until the next morning, Monday morning, an early Sunday night return was essential. The family's patience and stamina usually wilted by early evening — before supper — which meant Mr and Mrs Beaumont were alone in the house until we got home.

And when we got home we felt guilty all over again. Because without someone else in the house to prepare it, a hot meal on Sunday night was impossible. For people accustomed to a three-course supper by candlelight, served at the table, course-by-course, with wine, they were a sad Sunday night sight sitting at their bare table eating the cold simple supper I had prepared for them in advance.

Their pleasure at seeing us return was genuine — almost childlike — and impossible for them to conceal. Mrs Beaumont in particular wanted to know where we had been and what we had seen and done, and her enthusiasm and interest remained high while Kath helped her to bed.

So while I spent some time returning the kitchen to order, in readiness for a new week, Kath assumed her duties at the end of an exciting but tiring day. It was supposed to have been our day, a day to do as we wished, free of duties of any sort, but it ended for Kath as every other night did: acting as Mrs Beaumont's maid.

Chapter XX

IT WAS A DARK AFTERNOON. I WAS WORKING quietly in the kitchen, preparing for tea which had to be served at four o'clock.

I could hear a thunderstorm grumbling somewhere in the distance. Then, a flash of lightning; its light filled the kitchen. And then, before the thunder arrived, a sudden, horrible, shocking clanging noise. It terrified me. It was an alarm bell. Like a fire alarm but louder. Louder than I had ever heard. And it was in the house.

Was there a fire?

I dashed out of the kitchen trying to find the source of the noise; a nasty, jangling, piercing, emergency-type noise. Upstairs somewhere. Then, at last, the thunder. Deep. Banging repeatedly on the house. I leaped up the stairs. The bell noise grew louder. I ran around to the next flight and up to the ground floor. There I found Mr Beaumont. He was at the open front door. With Kath. The noise was horrible, frightening, painful in my ears. And the rain was sweeping in through the open door.

Lightning snapped and crackled. More banging thunder.

'Burglar alarm,' Kath mouthed to me behind Mr Beaumont's back, pointing with finger stabs to a small floor-level cupboard to one side of the door, a cupboard I had never before noticed. Mr Beaumont, though, was ignoring the cupboard — the source of the noise — and was fiddling with one of the door locks. More lightning. Thunder. Driving rain. Wet floor. And still the awful bell.

'What is it?' I shouted.

'Damned burglar alarm,' he shouted back through the noise, still fiddling with the lock. Waves of rain were driving into the house, soaking his lower trouser legs. He was standing in a puddle of water and I noticed for the first time that the lock he was playing with was wired. The thought of him playing with live wires in the driving rain did not appeal. What if I had to give him mouth-to-mouth resuscitation?

Another bang of thunder.

Ignoring him, and trying to ignore the pain in my ears, I stooped to the little cupboard. It was locked. I stood up.

'Where's the key?' I shouted in his ear.

He turned to face me.

'What key?'

Then he turned his ear to me to hear my reply.

'The key to the cupboard,' I shouted.

He pulled the chain from his waistcoat pocket. I discovered then that his chain did not carry a watch — as I had always assumed — but a large ring of keys. All his locking-up keys.

'Here,' he shouted, trying to turn the key-ring off the chain.

Ignoring his feeble efforts I took the ring from him and removed it from the chain. Still the horrible bell jangled in my ears.

By now Mrs Beaumont had come down for tea and she and Kath stood in the background, their hands covering their ears.

More crackling lightning. The crash of thunder following at once. And the rain. Driving in the open door onto the polished parquet floor. Kath pushed back the floor rug with her foot.

I dashed his hands away from the wired lock.

'Don't play with the wires,' I shouted, pointing down to the wet floor. 'It's dangerous. Electricity.'

He pulled a frightened face, understanding at once, embarrassed, and stepped back. I kneeled and tried the keys, all of them, but none worked.

'It's not here,' I shouted up to him. By now he, too, was standing back from the scene with his hands over his ears.

'What?' he shouted through the noise of the torrential rain, removing his hands from his ears.

'It's not here. The key's not here.'

'Lost,' he shouted down at me. 'Don't need it. The alarm's disconnected. Doesn't work.'

He put his hands over his ears again.

'Well it bloody well works now, you silly old bastard,' I said, not quietly.

I leaped down the stairs to fetch the old toolbox which was stored in the coal cellar. I chose a large screwdriver and used it to force open the little cupboard door. Then the noise was even louder. Inside the cupboard a large factory-sized red alarm bell was mounted on the wall, and a curved hammer, moving in a blur, was making the terrible noise. I jammed the screwdriver between the bell and the hammer and suddenly reduced the noise to a mere dull drilling.

I looked around and up to see the three of them looking down at me. Kath was smiling, amused, her hand to her mouth, but Mr and Mrs Beaumont look frightened. In shock.

Now what? I said to myself. My ears were aching — ringing — from the noise. But the thunderstorm had passed and it had nearly stopped raining. I stood up, the screwdriver in my hand.

'The house was struck by lightning,' I said, more to Mrs Beaumont than the dumbfounded old man. 'It must have shorted the alarm. How do we turn it off?' I asked, turning to him.

'Doesn't work,' he said. 'Disconnected years ago.'

Doesn't work. Disconnected.

I kneeled to the cupboard again. Ignoring the whirring noise I examined the workings of this ancient and very connected and very much working installation. The bell was wired to the mains through a timer switch or something. I tried the switch but nothing happened. There was also a conventional wall switch, like a light switch, and I tried that without success. An old-fashioned telephone without a dial was also wired into the alarm. Thinking that safe I yanked it out of its terminal but it made no difference to the vibrating hammer. Obviously the alarm had been designed to be tamper proof and I didn't want to start playing with the mains wiring. There was a badge with the name and phone number of the alarm company; I recognised the name but could tell by the phone number — the number of digits — that it, the phone number, was very old. Obsolete.

'I'll stay here,' I said to Kath. 'But could you go and phone the company—' I showed her the name '— and see what we should do. You'll have to look up the number. Maybe they'll send someone around to disconnect it.'

I found a rag in the toolbox and jammed it in beside the screwdriver so that the noise was thoroughly muffled. I stood up, moved to shut the front door, and found a helmeted policeman in a dripping-wet cape standing on the step. On this occasion Mr Beaumont was happy to let me deal with the situation.

'Is everything all right, sir?' he asked.

The rain had eased somewhat so I went outside with the constable, while Mrs Beaumont and a wet Mr Beaumont moved into the living room, and explained the situation to him as best I could.

'I didn't even know there was a burglar alarm in the house. But I know now.'

'Good idea to have a burglar alarm around here, mate,' said the policeman. And then, for the first time, I noticed that a small crowd had gathered at the front gate.

'Move along nah, ladies and gentlemen,' said the policeman as he ambled off. 'S'all over nah. Nuffink to see.'

But it was not all over for me.

The alarm company arrived before long and the serviceman was amazed at what he saw.

'Bleedin' fing's older 'n me,' he said. 'H'aint seen nuffink like it in all me all me born days.'

Evidently the alarm, which Mr Beaumont thought had been disconnected years ago, and so didn't work, had been only partially disarmed; the lightning storm had set it off somehow. But it was an obsolete model and even the serviceman couldn't turn it off and reset it. He could do nothing but disconnect it from the mains, rendering it permanently useless.

Meanwhile Kath had served tea and the house had returned to normal. But I was called to the living room by Mr Beaumont, who had changed into dry trousers, socks and shoes. He wanted to talk about the burglar alarm, blaming me for having had it disconnected. Despite the fact that it had been disconnected so long ago that he had forgotten about it, and that he had been without it for more years than he could remember, he now felt vulnerable without it

'Didn't have to turn it off,' he said from the comfort of his armchair.

'It was broken; it didn't work anyway,' I said patiently.

'Look here,' he said. 'Live in London now. Not the damn colonies you know. Need a burglar alarm. Everyone knows that. Should get the doings fixed.'

I was indifferent to his verbal abuse. Immune. I really didn't care. I knew that the alarm company wouldn't fix the old thing, and that for me to arrange a replacement would be futile. But without the comfort of the burglar alarm — a burglar alarm that didn't work and was forgotten anyway — Mr Beaumont became paranoid about security and even more vigilant in his evening locking up. And in the process he implied — constantly — that it would be my fault if the house were burgled.

When next I was in Kensington High Street I visited the alarm company and arranged for a salesman to phone the house to make an appointment to discuss a new installation. Knowing how such companies work I took great pains to ensure that high-pressure selling would not be used. I wanted an installation that was no more than the minimum necessary to put Mr Beaumont's mind at rest.

But nothing happened. I could only guess that by the time the company phoned to see him Mr Beaumont's anxiety attack had subsided. But the alarm episode, and the alarm itself, became another couple of things which I could not forget but which he could not remember.

Chapter XXI

'TEA AT FOUR,' CELIA HAD SAID.

Accordingly Mrs Beaumont rose from her afternoon nap and with Kath's help prepared herself for the rest of the day. Slowly and methodically she redressed, brushed her hair, applied fresh makeup, and descended on the electric chair to greet her husband who was by then rousing himself sleepily from his own siesta in the living room.

Meanwhile, and feeling somewhat refreshed, I went down to the kitchen to prepare the tea service, readying myself for the supper preparations which had to start immediately after tea; I knew it would be after nine o'clock, sometimes almost ten, before we would be able to return to our room.

'Tea' required more than just a cup of traditional hot English tea with milk and sugar. It was more of a ritual; a lavish Famous Five affair. The tea itself was taken with thinly-sliced lemon and had to be served with a silver tea service, a china tea set kept for the purpose, and china cake-plates loaded with as many and as much variety of cakes and biscuits as they could possibly carry.

I had quickly decided that the factory-made biscuits and cakes to which Mr and Mrs Beaumont had become accustomed — presumably given no choice by their staff — were less than appropriate and so I set about filling, and keeping full, the nested storage tins with my own home-made goodies. I chose old-fashioned recipes that I thought were traditionally English: neenish tarts, Afghans, little iced Queen cakes and big banana cakes, even New Zealand Anzacs and more. They were all immediately popular.

I did the baking once a week with pleasure and an irrational sense of satisfaction which was enhanced when we discovered the pride with which Mrs Beaumont offered the little home-made delicacies to her occasional tea guests. Little did she or they know that my inspiration was uniquely New Zealand and very prosaic. Called, plainly, *The Edmond's Cook Book* (first published in 1907, revised and reprinted many times), and consistently ranking as the biggest-selling book in New Zealand, it still bursts with homely kitchen advice, and recipes for cooking everything from pipis to pumpkins, possums to pork. It was also brimming with recipes for all the old-fashioned cakes and biscuits which were taken to New Zealand by British settlers, adopted as their own by New Zealand housewives, but apparently lost to the home-baking sisterhood of Britain. Thus its very old-fashionedness was the reason for its usefulness; the recipes it contained carried the textures, tastes and aromas of the past, the England of Mrs Beaumont's childhood.

But despite Mr and Mrs Beaumont's enjoyment of their afternoon tea it was in fact an elaborate and unnecessary meal that merely served to fill in time as well as filling their stomachs and so dulling their appetites for supper. Mr Beaumont in particular had an irresistible craving for sweetness which, even before his afternoon tea, he greedily gratified on his own, sitting alone in the living room chewing toffees retrieved from a secret source. He then stuffed the waxy wrappers down the side of the couch cushions in the belief that no-one would discover his vice. But Mariana always found the wrappers in the course of her work and disposed of them discreetly.

'Is not good for him to eat it so much the sweetis,' she said.

Usually there was just Mr and Mrs Beaumont for tea but occasionally there was a guest: sometimes Hermione or Alice called, or Julian, or, less frequently, a friend of Mrs Beaumont. But they were never spontaneous visits — not done to or by anyone in Mrs Beaumont's circle of friends and family — and in the case of friends were always the result of a written invitation.

I knew this because one of my morning chores — part of my shopping outing — was to post Mrs Beaumont's letters and I almost always recognised the name of a visitor from a letter posted only a day or two before. We also realised that these afternoons must have once been even more formal, with many more guests, when we found a cache of printed 'at home' cards. Larger than I expected, about the size of a postcard but white, they were formally printed in stark black:

Mr & Mrs H.O.H. Beaumont

AT HOME

The bottom left-hand corner carried the address in The Little Boltons, an obsolete telephone number, and an R.S.V.P. request.

But the days of 'At Home' formal teas were gone. Now tea was a more humble affair; and we were always given plenty of warning about expected guests.

'Lady So-and-so will be here for tea, dear,' Mrs Beaumont would say to Kath at their morning meeting and before long we recognised this as a coded request to put on our best show and deliver my very freshest cakes and biscuits. Thus did Kath answer the door, always just a minute or two before the appointed time of four o'clock, usher the Lady So-and-so into the living room, and quietly withdraw to give a stage-whispered shout down the stairs that they were ready for their tea.

For my part I had polished all the silverware that morning, a weekly chore, selected special china, and made an extra effort to prepare freshly-made treats — pikelets and Devonshire teas, with jam and lashings of whipped cream, were both favourites — to impress the guest. Mrs Beaumont, though, feigned indifference to our efforts on these special occasions seeking to suggest to her guest that such things were merely routine at The Little Boltons.

Knowing it would be some minutes before tea was served I had to get my timing perfect in order to have freshly boiled water ready at just the right moment. Then, on cue from Kath, and with The Monster loaded with everything but the teapot and extra boiling water, I quickly completed the tea-making ritual, loaded the teapot and water, and launched The Monster to the room above. Meanwhile Kath remained lurking outside the living room, waiting for the sound of The Monster arriving, at which moment she would enter the living room and begin serving tea with as much aplomb as she could muster, withdrawing again only when she sensed that Mrs Beaumont was satisfied that everything was in order and that conversation could begin.

Mr Beaumont's presence on these special occasions seemed only incidental; he simply had no recognised role in the ritual. Bored and hungry, he slumped into a sulk, drooling over the better-than-normal spread, eventually consuming its delights to the very limits of etiquette. Indeed it saddened him immensely if Mrs Beaumont ordered the tea things cleared before her visitor had left. A less inhibited man might have excused himself from the ladies' company and sneaked off to where conspiratorial servants would willingly have set aside a little personal feast especially for him. Instead he suffered these afternoons, frustrated by his latent good manners, and happy only when a guest left early and he could relieve his boredom by tucking into whatever remained on the plates.

By five, an hour after it had begun, the whole tea ritual was over. Meanwhile we managed to have a cup of tea of our own in the kitchen before clearing the living room and doing the dishes. Then it was time to start preparing supper. Although it wouldn't be required for two-and-a-half hours I would need all that time to prepare their three courses and, in the process, set aside something for ourselves which we would eat, when we could, Mr and Mrs Beaumont's own demands permitting.

Meanwhile they sat in the living room, until supper, doing I knew not what.

Chapter XXII

MR AND MRS BEAUMONT AND THEIR GUESTS weren't the only people to enjoy my baking.

In nineteen-ninety-two the Royal Borough was one of those parts of London which still had a remarkable range of people to provide whatever goods and personal services 'madam' might find necessary. Many of the callers to The Little Boltons were kind, sincere and pleasant people who had been calling at the house long enough to have developed what seemed to be a genuine concern for the owners upstairs. And yet as they invariably called to the area door — the tradesmen's entrance — and often dealt only with the cook, me, some of them had never met the old people upstairs whom they had served for so many years and for whom they expressed such deep concern. But their anxiety seemed real enough and only a complete cynic would have called it cupboard love.

Most of them — those who had been calling for many years — were as familiar with the house routines as we were. Each had a distinctly different mission and seemed programmed to arrive and depart — daily, weekly, fortnightly, monthly or six-weekly — according to some order laid down in the distant past; an arrangement which they had inherited and seemed reluctant to change or even question. Whether their sometimes dubious services were still required didn't seem to be an issue. They came because they had always come and were paid because they had always been paid. And the Beaumonts seemed as powerless to question the arrangements as they were. It all seemed silly and wasteful to me but my opinion was never sought and so was never given.

For example the Rentokil exterminator man called at the downstairs door every six weeks. He was a round, jolly-faced, pleasant sort of chap who always smiled, had a kind word, and always asked after the welfare of Mr and Mrs Beaumont.

'Been coming here thirty year now,' he told me with the hint of a West Country accent. 'You get attached to a family after all that toime.'

He wore a uniform of sorts and reminded me of Benny Hill, the television comedian, so we secretly called him Benny. He put down his bag of chemicals and equipment inside the area door and stopped to have a short chat. I half-expected him to give me a grinning, flat-handed salute across his forehead before carrying on with his work.

Benny didn't seem the sort of man to dedicate himself to the destruction of that which is indestructible but he told me that pest control and destruction was his life's work. He wandered around the neighbourhood by foot, carrying his collection of lethal chemicals, spending an hour or so in our house squirting and spraying around the basement floor and setting bait in cupboards and corners. It had must have worked because I never saw any sign of vermin or insect life — friend or foe — anywhere in the house.

Presumably there was once a problem. I didn't know exactly when but Benny told me that the company's records of the house went back to the nineteen-fifties. Clearly there was no problem in nineteen-ninety-two, and whether it was necessary for him to come quite so often, if at all, I had no idea. It was another case of no one questioning the arrangement and Mr Beaumont paying for something he probably didn't need. For my part I didn't like to think of how many hundreds of litres of chemicals had been sprayed around the house over the previous forty-odd years.

Benny immediately set about his grim work and was finished in an hour or so. But most of the other workers who called to the house — there was someone almost every day — followed what seemed to be an English worker's convention, certainly well-established at The Little Boltons, that absolutely no work could begin until one had sat in the kitchen for an hour or so talking to cook and enjoying a cup of hot milky tea. Unfortunately for me these workers happily helped themselves to the freshly-baked biscuits and cakes that were waiting in the tins; they considered the consumption of these delicacies — now home-made, fresh and delicious — to be one of the fringe benefits of their work. Their strategies varied but, somehow, they always ended up at the kitchen table lingering over their tea, biscuits and cakes.

I enjoyed their talk, and their indiscreet revelations about the family which was their employer — whose tea, biscuits and cakes they were so obviously enjoying — and their other clients in the neighbourhood but I was frustrated and annoyed by their assumption that I was there to cook for them. I quickly learned to keep aside items that were less than perfectly fresh, or less popular upstairs, for the nourishment of these hungry workers. In this way I could stop and listen to their stories without worrying about how quickly my best and freshest stores were being depleted.

Mr Larkin, the window cleaner, was typical of the paid-by-the-hour workers who called to the house to work but seemed to spend more of their paid time with me, in the kitchen, than they did at their assigned task. We always called him Mr Larkin because at our first meeting he said with great formality and dignity: 'Hi'm Mr Larkin and hi've been cleaning Mr Beaumont's winders since arfta the war.'

Mr Larkin had many strange tales to tell, as he sat in the kitchen enjoying his tea and cakes, but he rambled a lot and it was difficult to either date the stories or know when one finished and another began. He was a tall, rangy, bandy-legged old man with a large nose, transparent skin which had gone blotchy, a wet mouth missing many teeth, a bald pate that was inexplicably scarred and scabby and was bordered by a semicircle of long, stringy, grey hair that shot out in all directions. He always wore a white collarless shirt, a ragged three-piece navy-blue pinstripe suit, and scuffed black leather boots. He reminded me of an old Fagin although he was scrupulously honest and seemed to have a personal relationship with Mr Beaumont.

He told us that he lived with his wife at nearby and oddly-named World's End. He made his way around the Royal Borough, from one customer to the next, on a vintage black bicycle. His riding was remarkably straight given his advanced age, his bandy legs, and the fact that he carried his wooden ladder over his right shoulder from the end of which dangled a tin bucket full of his cleaning fluids and rags. It always amused me that he chained his bicycle to the iron fence outside the house with a security chain and lock that looked more valuable than the bicycle itself.

Mr and Mrs Beaumont didn't seem to notice but Mr Larkin was the only window cleaner I have known who managed to leave his 'winders' dirtier than they were before he began. Those that could be seen and reached were always re-cleaned by Mariana.

Daisy the gardener was another caller who always came to the downstairs door, for her hot cuppa and cookies, before beginning her work. She was always especially hungry and spent more time than most at the kitchen table. Despite her appropriate name Daisy told me she was in fact an artist — a sculptor— which meant I suppose that she had about as much right to call herself a gardener as I had to call myself a cook. But she called herself a gardener and had many gardening customers around the neighbourhood.

Daisy had the potential of great beauty but her mouth had been thinned and her brow furrowed by some internal worry. About thirty, she was small and delicate — not the gardener type at all — with an English-rose look about her complexion, especially in the winter when her cheeks turned rosy. Despite her small size her clothes were bulky and unflattering. She wore round, steel-rimmed glasses behind which her eyes darted about as if she were frightened of something. Indeed, she seemed to do everything with short, sharp, jerky movements. She even spoke that way, spitting out words and phrases as if she had a mouthful of dirt. She had an unusual accent, too, but I couldn't pick its origin.

From her attitude to the Beaumonts, the house, us, and her work, I had the impression that Daisy enjoyed her independence and was proud of being self-employed — her own boss — with customers of quality and standing; I don't believe she could ever have worked for wages, or would have bothered to dress better to please others, or to be pleasant to people like us. It was a pity. I wished she would relax so I could have come to know her better. But I guessed that this English class business was getting in the way, even between gardener and cook, although I couldn't tell if Daisy thought she was my superior or inferior; I suspect she thought she was somewhat superior.

Once she had enjoyed her luxurious tea, at her employer's expense, Daisy put a lot of work into the garden and on fine days spent as much time as necessary going around the garden slowly with Mrs Beaumont. In this she was always kind and patient, carrying out the pruning, thinning and moving work under her employer's direction, taking care to ensure, above all, that Mrs Beaumont would later be happy with what she would see from inside.

There were other workers of the 'upstairs' variety who never ventured downstairs. These callers considered themselves above us — metaphorically as well as physically — so we saw little of them although we knew who they were and when they were there. Mrs Beaumont's hairdresser was one. She came to the house every fortnight and charged an outrageous forty pounds to snip away at an old lady's short and thinning hair. Then there was the chiropodist, the physiotherapist, the dressmaker and, as far as I know, Uncle Tom Cobleigh and all. Although they were distinguished from the downstairs callers by their direct access to the lady of the house, calling to the front door and rendering a personal service, they shared an English cultural craving for tea and biscuits that had to be satisfied before work could begin.

Unlike the downstairs callers, who sat with me in the kitchen drinking their tea from a mug and eating their biscuits sometimes directly from the tin, upstairs callers had to be furnished with their tea and biscuits on a tray, with the finest china, delivered to the room by Kath. This placed them at a considerable psychological advantage, at least in their own minds, over those of their colleagues who called only to the area door — and so had to drink their tea with the cook in the kitchen — for whom they had nothing but contempt.

This jostling for position in the household hierarchy was a drama that was played out every day. It must have been important to the people involved, in the context of their narrow lives and their work, but to us it appeared petty and absurd. It had probably been going on for generations before us and will probably continue for generations into the future. But it must inhibit industry and innovation and is no doubt, even now, contributing to Britain's commercial and social decline. No wonder that so many sensible working class people left this otherwise lovely country for places where such contests have no meaning.

We colonials have much to thank our forefathers for.

Chapter XXIII

AS WELL AS HIS PRE-LUNCH MADEIRA MR BEAUMONT always enjoyed a gin and tonic before his supper and wine with supper; and my innocent involvement and desire to help with both predilections — his gin and his wine — got me into unexpected and unpredictable difficulties.

Although he had a cabinet full of gin downstairs it was my job to keep the pantry stocked with tonic and his bar upstairs stocked with freshly-cut lemons. The current gin bottle was kept, with a few other mostly untouched spirits, in an antique and locked tantalus which stood in the corner of a shelf on the dining room cabinet. I'd never heard of a tantalus — which tempts by putting its contents on show but out of reach — but learned that it was named after the eponymous Greek god who was punished in Hades by having visible food and drink always just out of reach. I also learned that in English houses like The Little Boltons the use of a tantalus was a common precaution against dishonest servants who might want a tipple.

In this case the tantalus was an open-topped wooden case divided into six square bottle compartments. Beautifully made and polished, the wood was reinforced at the corners with engraved silver plate. Arching across the top, lengthwise, was a convenient carrying handle that doubled as a clever locking device. When locked, the handle remained fixed and upright over the contents making the opening or removal of any bottle impossible; when unlocked the handle could be pushed aside and the bottles removed. Unfortunately the handle of this particular tantalus had become loose at one end which meant that it was a sloppy fit and that the precision lock didn't work to protect the contents from theft. It also meant that it couldn't be picked up by the handle as the unequal bottle weights spoiled the balance making the case swing on the loose handle thus tipping the bottles out.

'Could you fix it, Bob?' asked Mrs Beaumont. She had discovered my modest ability as a handyman. 'Harold would be so pleased.'

So pleased. I thought that would make a nice change.

I had never seen a tantalus before and was fascinated by its design, age and history. I took a close look at the problem and decided that it would be easy to repair; the tool kit in the cellar contained all the tools I would need. But I had to take it to the kitchen to make the repair and, worse, its precious contents had to remain with it as the securing of the bottle necks was an essential part of the locking process. This put Mr Beaumont in a dreadful quandary: he wanted the lock fixed in order to prevent pilfering of its contents and yet, in order to have the lock fixed he had to turn over the tantalus and its contents to the very person he most suspected of being a potential thief.

I didn't care what he thought. You want me to fix it then hand it over. If you don't want to hand it over then I can't fix it. Over to you. He must have followed the same reasoning. He handed it over.

It didn't take long to make the repair. Then I lightly oiled the moving parts, polished the wood with some of Mariana's furniture polish, and cleaned the silver embellishments with my silver cleaner until the thief-proof case looked and worked as good as new. Then I returned the untouched bottles to their compartments, secured the handle in place over their necks, locked the whole affair and returned it upstairs with its key.

I found Mr Beaumont waiting anxiously for my return. He took the tantalus from me quickly — grabbing it rudely — checked the lock, removed the key, and only then expressed his gratitude with as little grace as he could, making it clear that any diminution of case's contents would be noticed.

But then, somehow, once I had left the room, he lost the key. The newly-renovated tantalus could not be opened. Now, against all his better judgement, he had to leave a new gin bottle standing, vulnerable and unsecured, on the cabinet shelf beside the locked tantalus.

Weeks later Mariana found the missing key behind the cabinet where he must have dropped it. Until then I suspect he checked the level of the unsecured gin bottle every morning. With a clear conscience, and the knowledge that his complaints of liquor-stealing by staff had always been ignored by the members of the families, his silly suspicions didn't concern me.

But it wasn't long before he openly accused me of stealing his wine.

Mr Beaumont took a lot of pride in his wine cellar which was in fact a large steel cabinet lined with wine racks and sealed with a heavy padlock. When he came downstairs to choose a wine for supper he often showed me the cabinet's contents and discussed his wine preferences. He did not, he told me bluntly, like French wines (probably because they were French), red wines or dry wines. The fact that these plainly stated dislikes, alone or in any combination, ruled out most of the world's finest wines didn't seem to bother him. And his less than catholic tastes seemed odd in a man who was so proud of his membership of The Worshipful Company of Vintners.

Instead, he insisted, he liked sweet German wines and I knew that the cellar's contents consisted entirely of certain and not always good Hocks and Moselles. In this I knew he was conforming to the obsolete fashion for the old *Hochheim* wines, set by Queen Victoria and her German husband, thus perhaps choosing not what he liked but what he thought he *should* like.

Incidentally, my keen interest in his wine cellar touched a rare soft spot and sometimes, while Kath and I were gulping our dinner in the kitchen, and the Beaumonts were eating supper above us, he would use The Monster to send down two glasses of warm Hock. Kath always thanked him accordingly.

Mr Beaumont told me he had a wine agent in Bristol who imported his wine, sherry and Madeira especially for him and every now and then I had to take front-door delivery of a carton or two from Bristol which he got me to take downstairs. Afraid of leaving them entirely in my care for even a moment he would follow me down, painstakingly open the cartons and immediately store the bottles in the cellar's racks.

I was surprised, therefore, when early one Thursday evening there was a ring at the area door and a local supplier, whose shop I knew well, delivered two mixed cartons of wine. I looked inside and found a selection of some of the finest and most expensive clarets.

French, red and dry? It didn't make sense.

'Are you sure?' I asked. It was the proprietor himself making the delivery; I knew him from my visits to his Hollywood Road shop to buy much less expensive wines than these for our own enjoyment.

'Oh, yes,' he said. 'Mr Beaumont chose the wines himself.'

'When?'

'This afternoon.'

A Thursday afternoon. After his visit to town and his club.

'He chose them himself? You didn't help him?'

'No. Why? Is something wrong?'

'Yes,' I said, puzzled but reluctant to explain something so complicated. 'But it's not your fault.'

'But— '

'Look,' I said. 'If he doesn't want these, if he changes his mind, could he exchange them?'

'Of course. But for what?'

'He really prefers German wines, white and sweet,' I said. '*Qualitätswein* even. I don't know why he chose these. It could be a mistake.'

But the biggest mistake was mine. I should never have got involved.

Mr Beaumont's doctor had ordered him to walk more, and suggested that he could start on Thursday afternoons, on the way home from town, by having the taxi drop him in Fulham Road whence he could make the short walk home. Somehow, on this particular Thursday, he had been drawn into the wine shop and had made his mysterious purchase of French dry red wines.

'Look here,' he said when I showed him the wine. 'Never been in that shop in my life. Not mine.'

He pulled one of the dark and unfamiliar bottles out of the carton and examined the label closely.

'French.' He appeared disgusted. 'Never drink the stuff. Get rid of it. Not mine.'

'But you signed for it,' I said, showing him the invoice he had signed himself.

'Rubbish,' he said, not bothering to look at the evidence. 'Get rid of it.'

The next day at the wine shop I explained the problem as discreetly as I could and the proprietor let me choose something more suitable. He said he would deliver it to the house and pick up the unwanted *Bordeaux*. And to make things simple he said he would destroy the original invoice and issue a new one for the new amount.

So I chose what I considered a suitable and familiar-looking *Rheingau* which arrived the next day in two sealed cartons. Unable to enter the steel cellar myself I left the cartons standing beside the door for Mr Beaumont. When he found them, however, he didn't remember how or why they were there. Nor did he remember the original discussion about the French wine. The only conclusion he could reach — a logical conclusion given his grasp of the 'facts' as he knew them — was that I had ordered these two sealed cartons for myself. Unfortunately but inevitably the new invoice, billed to him, had my signature on it.

He immediately accused me of theft and at first I defended myself vigorously. But it was impossible; he remembered nothing of what he did and what had happened. He believed I was a thief and said so to anybody who happened to visit upstairs. Of course nobody took any notice of him — they had all heard it all before — but he persisted with the accusations for weeks.

Meanwhile, unwilling to get further involved, I left the wine cartons where they stood. Eventually he came across them again and apparently forgetting all that had gone before decided to open them and store the bottles. But he couldn't manage to break the carton seals, and wouldn't ask me for help, so they remained outside the cellar door until eventually we all got sick of tripping over them and I put them in the coal cellar.

They're probably still there.

Chapter XXIV

'SUPPER AT SEVEN-THIRTY,' CELIA HAD SAID.

While at home in New Zealand I could rustle up a nourishing hot meal for the family in half-an-hour or so, supper, as the evening meal was called at The Little Boltons, required meticulous planning.

It started at the meeting Kath had with Mrs Beaumont in her study each morning. The menu for supper was the first priority. Mrs Beaumont's decision on this weighty matter was always steered by Kath who was in turn steered by me in a direction that depended on a number of things: the contents of the pantry, whether it was a grocery-ordering Tuesday, or whether or not I wanted, or had time, to make a walking journey to the supermarket or the street market.

Three courses were required each evening — accompanied by Mr Beaumont's favourite sweet German wine for which he made a special trip downstairs each day — served and eaten by candlelight, always dark green candles, on a perfectly set table. And serving had to begin at precisely seven-thirty.

Advance planning helped and once I was familiar with their particular favourites I made sure I over-made and committed the surplus to the freezer for a later occasion. Steak and kidney pudding was a firm favourite, and because their portions were so small it was sensible and economical to make three or four puddings at the same time. When Mrs Beaumont next required steak and kidney pudding I felt as though I was on holiday.

The house was a lucrative source of business for many of the tradesmen suppliers of the area. Business was still conducted in the old-fashioned way: that is, the house could and did phone and order anything it liked, or needed, at will, and the supplier undertook to deliver it to the door. Money was never discussed but a bill was enclosed with the delivery and a statement was rendered by mail at the end of the month. It was my job to collect these bills until the end of the month, Mrs Beaumont's to approve them by reconciling them with the appropriate statement, and Mr Beaumont's duty to pay them. So far as I know he never questioned the number or size of the bills — didn't even look at them — but paid them promptly and without question by personal cheque.

When it came to buying food and housekeeping provisions, which were Mrs Beaumont's financial responsibilities, she used this system to her own financial advantage, conserving her cash reserves. Because although I could easily walk to the twenty-four-hour food markets in Fulham Road, Sainsbury's in Cromwell Road, or to the nearby North End market, and pay much less than what was asked by the customary suppliers, I would require cash which Mrs Beaumont would have to give me from her own housekeeping fund. Therefore, despite the much greater cost of home delivery by the traditional suppliers, she found it more economic, at least in terms of her own housekeeping budget, to use credit and leave her husband to pay the inflated monthly accounts as he did each month without question.

Large orders were placed with a Fulham Road grocer who had a tiny nineteenth century shop. How, I wondered, could he stock and supply such a variety as that which Mrs Beaumont ordered and they delivered? I once spoke to one of the staff, without identifying myself, and learned that the shop had once carried everything it needed, storing it in the basement. But now, he said, it was not economic to carry the vast range of imported and expensive delicacies ordered by their wealthy customers. I noticed for example that they didn't even have tonic water and yet they delivered a carton to the house every week.

So what did they do? I began checking prices and the answer became obvious: they simply went up or down the road, to one or other of the modern mini-markets, buying what they needed at retail and plussing it up on their own invoice knowing that their customers would have no idea of the usual price. In this way they not only made a profit on the sale they also reduced their inventory and storage overheads to almost zero. And then they audaciously charged for delivery.

The butcher was especially interesting. Although the shop was small the owners claimed — by a sign in the window — to have their own beef, sheep, pig and poultry farms (chickens and ducks) although it seemed unlikely to me that such a small shop would be able to own and profitably manage so many farming enterprises. Perhaps they had other branches but that too seemed unlikely; it was clearly a small family business and looked likely to have been in the same family for generations. Whatever the source of their meat, though, I can confirm that it was superior to anything I found anywhere in London. I'm sure it was also the most expensive meat in the world.

For example the Beaumonts enjoyed a roast chicken and, except for their favourite sauce, I enjoyed cooking it for them. On chicken day Mrs Beaumont phoned the butcher herself and within an hour or so there would be a ring at the area door and a mysterious gentleman in a white coat and panama hat would hand over a plain white plastic bag in which rested the required bird; cool, moist, heavy and plump.

The charge, on the hand-written invoice at the bottom of the bag, was five or six pounds plus a round pound for delivery, a total sum which I found obscenely large when we related it to the costs we were used to at home; at that time we could buy a large chicken for the equivalent of two pounds, about the same price as that ruling at an English supermarket.

Despite its absurdly high cost the butcher's chicken was so poorly cleaned and dressed it looked awful. It took me a long time to cut off the scaly yellow lower legs, clean it properly inside and out, and pluck the many remaining quills one at a time with a pair of needle-nosed pliers. It was an awful and seemingly unnecessary job.

I once challenged the butcher about it; the glass display was full of these fully-legged, badly-dressed and feathery birds.

'Our customers like them that way,' he said.

'Why?'

'It proves they're not from the supermarket,' he replied.

'You mean— '

He waited. But I surrendered. Perturbed. Thinking again, as I often did in this peculiar country, how strange and upside-down it was that the best and most expensive product — the butcher's five or six pounds worth of chicken (plus one pound delivery) — was intentionally presented badly in order to better demonstrate its superiority.

Evidently it was better because it looked worse.

Ironically, if other houses were like ours, the buyer of the chicken never saw the uncooked bird anyway and so never saw how awful it looked to infer how superior it surely must be.

'Could Bob make us some bread sauce?' Mrs Beaumont asked Kath at one morning menu meeting when chicken was being put on the menu. Apparently she and her husband liked bread sauce with chicken.

'Of course,' Kath replied.

'Bread sauce?' I asked.

'Bread sauce,' said Kath.

'What the hell is bread sauce?'

She shrugged.

'We'll look it up.'

So we looked it up in a nineteen-fifty edition of Marguerite Patton's *Recipes For The Modern Housewife* — a book I had found in the kitchen — and I couldn't believe what I read. So I checked it in my Edmond's book and there it was: bread sauce is made by sticking a clove — one clove — into a peeled onion and resting the said cloved onion in a cup of cold milk. After an unspecified time in the cold milk — Edmond's said to simmer it for a while, Marguerite Patton didn't — the onion and clove are removed, apparently disposed of, never to be seen again; the resulting 'flavoured' milk is then heated to a simmer. Breadcrumbs are added and the simmering continued until the sauce thickens at which time butter, salt and pepper are added, and then water to get the just the right consistency, whatever that might be.

'It's bread and milk,' I said indignantly, not believing that any meaningful flavour could migrate from clove to onion and then from onion to milk.

'It's English,' said Kath defensively.

'It's bloody awful.'

'It's English,' again, as if that explained everything.

'And what about the onion? I thought onions were banned.'

That was the rule. No onions in the house. And no garlic. Evidently, according to Mariana, when Mrs Beaumont was still active and in charge of the kitchen she once discovered garlic in the pantry. From there, up the hall and into the kitchen she marched, holding the large, white, papery-covered clump out at a stiff-arm's length, while her nostrils were clamped tightly shut by the fingers of her other hand.

'What,' she demanded to know of the assembled staff, 'is this?'

Having been informed of its identity she promptly banned its use — even its presence — in the house. This ban had made such an impression on Mariana and her contemporaries that it had remained in force, becoming knitted into the fabric of downstairs folk history, passing from servant to servant for twenty-five years.

At first I put this anti-garlic attitude down to the gastronomic conservatism of Mrs Beaumont's generation but changed my mind — deciding it was a widely-held British opinion — when I read about growing garlic in a popular and contemporary English gardening book.

'Garlic,' it said, 'has an important role in Continental but not in British cookery. It really isn't worth growing unless you are a fan.'

It then went on to describe how to use garlic in cooking: 'If you are a beginner with garlic, you must use it very sparingly or you will be put off forever,' it said, and more. The section ended quaintly with the words: 'If by then you have lost a little of your garlic fear, you could try using crushed (not chopped) garlic in meat etc. as the Continentals do.'

The continental Mariana believed that the onion and garlic ban was still in force although she knew I used them liberally all the time, especially in my *lasagne,* and obviously onions weren't banned when it came to the bread sauce.

'So?' I asked again, 'what about the onion?'

But Kath had no answer because there could be no answer.

'Make it and shut up,' she said.

I made the bread sauce and it tasted exactly like—

'It's bread and milk,' I insisted.

'Well it's English and it's old and they like it,' said Kath. 'So serve it.'

I served it. I also made a stuffing of marjoram, thyme, sage and parsley mixed with eggs and thinned with some white German wine and a stock made from the chicken giblets. And I made gravy; real chicken gravy.

I thought everyone loved chicken gravy. But Mr and Mrs Beaumont ignored the gravy and didn't even discover the stuffing because Mr Beaumont didn't carve deeply enough into the breast. Indeed, of the entire expensive, hand delivered, hand-raised, hand plucked, double cleaned and dressed, free-range chicken worth five or six pounds — plus a pound for delivery — they each ate only a slice or two of breast hacked off by Mr Beaumont with a blunt knife.

But they devoured the bread sauce.

I didn't bother making gravy or stuffing after that; and I found instant bread sauce at the supermarket which saved time and released me from the embarrassment of having to take responsibility for such a colourless, odourless and tasteless sauce. And each week the remains of one of the world's most expensive chickens went into the pot to make a rich chicken soup, full of onion, or was turned into a chicken *fricassee,* also with plenty onion and some garlic, which they enjoyed and was ideal for weekend reheating. In fact I think they enjoyed the soup and the *fricassee* more than they enjoyed the original roasted bird.

But they *loved* the bread sauce.

Chapter XXV

A FISH SUPPER WAS REQUIRED ONCE A WEEK. AND fish was even more expensive than chicken or meat. The fishmonger gave a personal service by calling to the area door each week. His name was Billy and like the butcher's delivery man he had a plain white van and wore a white coat. He came to the door, jolly and red-faced, bouncing with enthusiasm and bursting to talk which he did in short, sharp sentences as if his enthusiasm and bounciness had left him breathless.

We let him into the kitchen and then we —Kath, Mariana and I — stood with him for ten minutes or so discussing the fish needs of the household, the quality of the North Sea catch, the condition of today's haddock, the Iceland question, the temperature of the rivers in Scotland during the past week, the effect of recent Atlantic storms and so on. It was all terribly serious and for the first time in my life I began to understand the significance of the question: 'What's that got to do with the price of fish?' As far as Billy the fishmonger was concerned, in the Royal Borough in nineteen-ninety-two, everything in the world had something to do with the price — the very high price — of English fish.

Once the expensive fish discussions were over, and decisions made, I followed Billy up to the street. We stood at the back of his van in The Little Boltons while he described the white, wet fish available on the day. The Beaumont's fish tastes were predictably conservative so it was always a choice between sole, plaice, haddock and cod although they frequently enjoyed Scottish smoked salmon — as deliciously tender, delicate and orange-pink as one would expect for the price — as an *entrée*, properly treating it as a luxury. But it made me homesick to think of the exquisite

South Island smoked salmon so taken for granted at home for only a fraction of the price. In fact the longer we remained in England — eating what the English ate and seeing what they had to pay — the more New Zealand seemed like food-lover's paradise.

Once I had made my decisions, and I learned from experience to trust Billy's recommendation, Billy weighed the fish on his suspended scales, added up the cost in his head, and I paid him in cash — no credit from Billy — from Mrs Beaumont's precious housekeeping fund. No receipt. No records. No questions. I kept careful notes of what I spent with Billy but an account of the fish expenditure was never required. But it was never less than thirty pounds — about ninety New Zealand dollars then — and it astonished me that the amount spent on fish for two old people with not large appetites was about the same as what we then spent at home for an entire week's worth of food.

Although Billy's fish was always meaty and fresh, and so a pleasure to prepare and cook, it was impossible for me to distinguish between the bland flavours of the various species. At first I thought it was because my tastes had been conditioned by different fish, or by the frequent consumption of strongly-flavoured New Zealand shell fish, but I changed my mind, deciding that fish flavour was not important to the English, when once we were in a fish and chip shop.

'What's the difference between cod and plaice?' Kath asked the chippy, innocently.

'Fifty pence, luv,' he said. 'It's on the sign.'

Whether the main course was meat, chicken or fish, vegetables were always served but as usual Mrs Beaumont's tastes were plain and undemanding while Mr Beaumont ate vegetables only reluctantly. At first I tried to introduce taste, variety and colour but soon learned that they didn't like any vegetable that was unfamiliar or familiar vegetables served in an unfamiliar way. And so I quickly decided to give them only what they knew. Even so I frequently got stumped by the most simple things. Like cabbage.

'They just don't like it,' said Kath.

Even my trusty Edmond's book didn't tell me how to cook cabbage to Mrs Beaumont's liking.

'Cabbage (shredded),' it said. 'Cook 8 to 10 mins. in a little boiling water.'

I tried everything which actually isn't much because there isn't much you can do with cabbage served plain. I was close when I stirred butter through it before serving but that worried me because I had been instructed to use butter only sparingly. I tried it with margarine but it wasn't the same, and the return of the almost-full dish told me it was not right anyway. Whatever I did the cabbage was always returned uneaten.

We had discovered a restaurant in Leicester Square notable for its authentic English cuisine. We went there one Saturday night. I ordered steak and kidney pudding — my own was easily as good, probably better — and cabbage. As soon as I tasted the cabbage I just about jumped out of my upholstered cubicle with joy; the excitement of discovery.

'This is absolutely horrible,' I said.

It was so horrible I couldn't eat it.

'It is so horrible it's perfect. Exactly right.'

I couldn't wait to cook cabbage again because I thought I knew what I'd been doing wrong. And I was right. The next time cabbage was served to the Beaumonts the serving dish was returned empty.

'Perfect,' said Kath, impressed. 'What did you do?'

'It was *so* obvious.'

'Was it?'

'Yes'

'What did you do?'

'Well first I chopped it up very small. Like it was at Porters.'

'Yes?'

'And then—'

'What?' She was getting impatient.

'—I cooked the shit out of it.' I said, smugly.

She laughed. 'How long?'

'Oh, hours.'

'Hours? How many hours?'

'How many hours from after lunch to supper?'

Kath counted, laughing. 'Five or six,' she said. 'About.'

'Well, five or six hours then,' I said. 'About.'

'That makes it worthless,' she said.

'I know,' I said. 'But they ate it. They bloody well ate it.' I was triumphant.

'So they did,' she said.

'Come on,' I said. 'Time for dessert.'

Chapter XXVI

HAVING EACH OF THE SUPPER COURSES READY AT the right time was the most demanding part of my work; knowing when to go up and into the dining room to clear the remains of each finished course and deliver the next was Kath's.

There was an old electric bell in the kitchen. It made a horrible sound but was set high above the stove out of reach of tampering servants. It and the one in our bedroom were all that remained of what was once a house-wide servant-summonsing system now activated only by the button beside Mrs Beaumont's bed — in case of emergency — and another in the dining room. Its purpose in the dining room was to signal to the kitchen staff that the diners above had finished their course.

Annoyed by the harsh sound of the bell, and with few intellectual challenges available, we took an absurd pride in providing a seamless dining service. We became so good at anticipating the needs of the diners above that the bell was made redundant, but Mr and Mrs Beaumont, for whose dining pleasure we made such an effort, seemed to take such a streamlined and one-to-one-ratio service for granted, commenting only when it was less than perfect.

It seemed never to occur to the diners to question quite how Kath — merely a slip of a maid from the 'colonies' — should know the precise moment her services were required in the dining room. They didn't realise that when The Monster was up, in the dining room, as it was between courses, the resulting 'hole' in the dining room floor/kitchen ceiling allowed us to guess by the sounds that drifted down to us — their conversation and the changing tones of silverware on china — exactly when Kath should return to clear the finished course and stand by for the delivery and serving of the next.

Our dinner in the kitchen was usually much the same as the supper being served upstairs, cooked at the same time, although its consumption was constantly interrupted by the needs of the diners upstairs. Whenever it was necessary Kath left her own dinner, dashed upstairs, glided silently into the dining room, cleared the table quickly, loaded The Monster, pressed its button, and so sent it down to me laden with empty serving dishes, soiled plates, glassware and cutlery, rattling, clinking and clanking together on their journey. The sudden stop at the bottom of the rails jarred everything noisily and bounced the iron counterweight that was by now hanging, at kitchen ceiling height, on its ancient steel cable. I then set aside my dinner to quickly replace the waiter's entire dirty contents with the next course.

Meanwhile, above, Kath fussed at the table, filling in time until, at my command, The Monster lumbered up through the floor again laden with some of the world's most expensive food.

Our professional objective was to minimise Kath's work, carrying plates and dishes unnecessarily up and down the stairs, by ensuring that The Monster was always loaded with everything necessary for each course. It was a lesson we had learned the hard way.

One night I had made a chocolate *mousse* for dessert. Because it was so rich, and decorated with sweetened whipped cream, I sent it up without the customary crystal jug of liquid cream. As usual I was standing beneath the hole to hear how the serving was progressing, and how the course was being appreciated, when I heard Mrs Beaumont's question to Kath.

'Is there any cream?'

'Cream?'

Kath was surprised by the request as the dessert was so obviously laden with whipped cream.

Stranded in the dining room, with no way of communicating to me but by an undignified and unacceptable shout down the hole in the floor, Kath was reduced to running down to the kitchen for the cream. Forewarned by my practised eavesdropping I met her half way with the required crystal jug of cream on a silver salver.

Always the professional, Kath re-entered the dining room, quietly, completely composed, presented the tray to Mrs Beaumont who took the jug wordlessly and passed it across the table to her husband.

'Cream, darling?' she asked.

'No, thank you,' he said without looking up.

'Not for me either, dear,' said Mrs Beaumont, handing the untouched cream jug to Kath who was still silently panting from the record-breaking dash down to the kitchen and back.

Listening below, I couldn't help laughing out loud.

'I heard you laughing,' said Kath when she returned to the kitchen.

But she was laughing, too. And 'cream, darling?' became our code, used just before the dinner service began, for 'Are you sure that absolutely nothing has been left off The Monster?'

Cold desserts were always a problem because they needed so much cooling time. It meant that the last course of the day was usually the one I had to prepare first in the morning, directly after breakfast.

The popular rhubarb fool was typical although the first problem was that neither of us had ever heard of rhubarb fool. Such a foolish name, I thought, although, as often happens, I then began seeing it and other fruity 'fools' everywhere. But it was simple enough to make being merely cold stewed rhubarb (or other cold stewed fruit) whipped into a vanilla-flavoured corn flour custard; as plain, simple and old-fashioned as a dessert could be. But having stewed the fruit first it took a lot of time to cool.

But no cold dessert took as long to prepare as summer pudding.

'I think we'll have a summer pudding tomorrow night, dear,' Mrs Beaumont said. 'Harold does like it so.'

Tomorrow night? Kath was nonplussed by such advanced warning. But, clearly, two days warning meant summer pudding obviously had to be prepared well in advance. The problem was that, like rhubarb fool, neither of us had ever heard of summer pudding.

Resourceful as ever, Kath had developed the perfect technique for such occasions. They were in the study for the usual morning meeting; Mrs Beaumont sat at her desk in her wheelchair while Kath sat to her left, a pad on her lap.

'Well,' said Kath, hiding her summer pudding ignorance, pencil poised over pad, ready with her trick. 'Everyone has their own favourite recipe for—' and here she inserted the desired dish, '—summer pudding. How do you like yours?'

Downstairs: 'They want summer pudding.'

'What?'

'Summer pudding,' she said again.

'What the hell's summer pudding?' I asked, reaching for my Edmond's.

'It's not in there,' she said. 'I looked.' She tapped the side of her head with her pencil. 'It's in here.'

'You didn't write it down?'

'Didn't have to. It's so simple.'

'Well it's not in the Edmond's book.'

'I told you. Doesn't matter. I know how to make it.'

'How?'

To make summer pudding requires plenty of fresh juicy fruit and berries; it seems that any fruit or berries will do but strawberries, raspberries and blackberries seem to be favourites. One then takes a pudding bowl and lines it completely with buttered white bread without crusts. The selected fruit is then dumped into the bowl and sealed over with more buttered white bread.

Marguerite Patton confirmed Kath's recipe.

'White bread? With butter?'

'Yes.'

'They're not supposed to have butter.'

'Too bad. She said butter so butter it is. Now listen will you. Here comes the tricky bit.'

The tricky bit?

A plate, slightly smaller than the diameter of the pudding bowl, is rested on top of the closing layer of bread, and on top of this plate one loads as much heavy weight as can be found. I used all the iron weights from the old-fashioned kitchen scales, nesting them one inside the other to make a little iron mountain weighing considerably more than two old-fashioned English pounds. All this weight, distributed evenly across the top of the pudding by the plate, presses out the juices from the fruit into the bread, saturating it and colouring it with its own bright and natural colour.

'That's it?'

'Well you have to chill it, and leave it for twenty-four hours to make sure all the juices come though. Then you tip it out of the bowl without breaking it.'

'The bowl?'

'No. The pudding. Don't break the shape of the pudding.'

'And that's it?'

'That's it.'

I thought about it.

'It's a jam sandwich.'

'It's what they want.'

So that's what they got.

I went to the North End market, carefully chose the berries with the most juice potential, bought some fresh, sliced, white bread, and began my first summer pudding.

But why 'summer pudding' I wondered. My guess was that prosperous Victorians or Edwardians, or their cooks, faced with an unprecedented abundance of home-grown berries, and new exotic berries and fruits from the empire, but unfamiliar with the delights (or benefits) of eating them raw, straight from tree or vine, were compelled to turn them into something they could recognise. And as they had always called the course after the main course 'pudding', and as it was always stodgy and cooked in a round pudding bowl, they did to that fresh summer fruit the only thing they knew: they put it into a pudding bowl, shaped it into a pudding shape, and called it a pudding. A summer pudding.

I watched the development of my first summer pudding, stored in the cool pantry, with an intense interest all that day and the next, looking forward to the moment when I could turn it out — without breaking it — in all its bread-and-buttery glory.

Despite the butter hardening somewhat in the cold, making some of the bread stick to the bowl, it retained the desired shape of an upside-down pudding bowl although an excess of juices needed to be drained off the plate before serving.

I set it in the middle of the kitchen table.

'Summer pudding,' I said to Kath and Mariana as we stood back to admire the ridiculous thing. They both clapped politely and I took a little bow.

As usual, however, I over-provided and the collapsed shape of its remains, when the plate came back to the kitchen, meant it wouldn't be fit to serve again.

'How did they like it?' I asked.

'They loved it. But what's it like?' Kath was as intrigued and amused by the thing as I was.

The non-pudding shape now didn't worry me as I dug in a spoon and tasted summer pudding for the first time.

'Well,' I said, tasting another spoonful and looking thoughtfully to the ceiling as if to concentrate on the flavours. 'Not bad really. It's like—'

'Like what?'

'It's like a bloody jam sandwich.'

Chapter XXVII

WHILE NOT OBSESSED WITH THE DISTANT AND unknown origins of my family name, which came to New Zealand via Ireland not England, I was intrigued — as were our friends and family — by the coincidence that we should be living and working in a place where the streets were named for the Bolton family upon whose farm they were built.

The Boltons, running parallel to The Little Boltons, was one of the most elegant avenues of the record reign. Its houses were mansions, on land more generous than the properties in The Little Boltons, with driveways and stables and detached cottages for servants set in spacious gardens. At one end, in the measured middle of its width and within a courtly iron-fenced ellipse, stood Saint Mary The Boltons, the little church whose grey spire we could see from our top-floor room across the ways.

There was a chipped and faded sign wired to the church's black iron fence. This fence was a relatively recent replacement for the original which was removed during the war by churchly patriots as a contribution to the country's drive for metal. Who knows into what great machine, armament, ordnance, ship, aeroplane, weapon or missile went that iron in the cause of war? And did anyone care, I wonder, that church materials were used for such an awful purpose?

It was not hard to find old survey maps in the library and I found that The Little Boltons had originally been named The Grove. My guess was that past residents had sought to enhance both their property values and their social standing by a closer association with the affluence and fame of their neighbouring street. Perhaps it worked because as far as I could tell most houses in The Little Boltons in nineteen-ninety-two were worth two or three million pounds.

On Bank Holiday weekends we were given time off from early Saturday morning until late Monday night and on one such rare weekend we extended our name associations with a two-and-a-half hour train trip north to Manchester where we planned to visit the town of Bolton. It was a cold miserable weekend but we enjoyed Manchester immensely, finding it a big, grand, Victorian city bursting with pride and Northern friendliness.

Like most visitors at that time we headed first to the Granada television studios for a tour of the Coronation Street set where we photographed ourselves in front of everything we recognised, ending our day 'wi' pint at Rover's'. And as an erstwhile viewer of the famous television programme Kath was amused to hear the accent of 'The Street' directed at her.

'Ee oop, chuck,' someone said to her in one Manchester shop. And when, at Ladbrokes the bookmakers, she placed a couple of bets on *Auntie Dot* and *Cool Ground* in the Grand National — knowing nothing of form and being accustomed to the computerised wizardry of the New Zealand totalisator — the bookmaker, handwriting her bet on a little pink slip, advised her to 'take summat each road, luv.'

'Aye,' I said to her. 'Happen each road's best, luv.'

I was intrigued to be in Manchester. Having once lived in the southern United States, and being especially interested in the antebellum culture there, the American Civil War, and the hundred-year-long civil rights campaign which followed it, I was intrigued to now be in the city which was once the world centre of the cotton industry. It was Manchester's mills that had once so fostered the Atlantic cotton trade, and the slavery it depended on, and whose later owners had joined the English anti-slavery movement.

We went on to Bolton — now no more than an independent borough of Manchester — with some trepidation. My paternal grandfather had visited there as a soldier on leave during the first world war and I remembered the stories he had told. To him Bolton represented all that was evil about England, the industrial revolution and the degradation it brought to the working classes of England's mill towns; the archetype dark, satanic mill town of

Victorian times; the very reason so many working people, our ancestors included, had left Britain for New Zealand.

I always supposed he had been exaggerating; surely, I thought, it couldn't have been as bad as he said. But even in nineteen-ninety-two the cramped terrace housing of England's industrial cities looked mean and nasty to us as it did to most New Zealanders. And the lifestyle of those who must live in these cities — in conditions that New Zealanders would consider completely unacceptable — is unimaginable in New Zealand. To my grandfather then, a young man born and raised in the nineteenth century New Zealand countryside, Bolton and towns like it must have looked like hell on earth when he was there in the second decade of the twentieth century.

We found the Manchester city bus depot easily enough and again I experienced the odd feeling of seeing my name everywhere, even on the bus. The journey to Bolton, in the Number 553 double-decker, was only short and we got off near the centre of town and spent an hour or so just wandering around. It was a pleasant experience. The town looked neat and prosperous — pretty even — with no evidence of the filth and ugliness described so vividly by my grandfather.

Bolton has a long history, and many famous sons and daughters. One of the most notable was Samuel Crompton whose spinning-mule, invented in 1799, brought wealth and fame to Bolton and ensured Lancashire's world leadership in cotton for the next hundred years. Mr W. H. Lever, later Lord Leverhulme, who was also born in the town, in 1851, went on to make his fortune based on the Sunlight Soap brand. Presumably his family had taken the name from the nearby village of Little Lever, the only town in the district mentioned in the Domesday Book.

The showpiece of Bolton though, without doubt, was the magnificent town hall. This imposing, towering, Victorian stone monument stood in the town centre surrounded by a paved pedestrian precinct. While we were admiring the building we were attracted by a fuss at the bottom of the steps. A limousine stood nearby, the only car in an otherwise car-less area, and a uniformed chauffeur was leaning on it, smoking, waiting.

Moving closer to the little gathering we could see that it was the start or finish of a cycle race. Photographs were being taken with

the riders and, in the centre of the hubbub, stood an important-
and distinguished-looking, silver-haired gentleman in a morning
suit with a chain of office draped over his shoulders.

'Is that the mayor?' I ask the chauffeur.

'Oh, aye,' he said. 'Lord Mayor.'

'Of Bolton?'

'Aye. Lord Mayor of Bolton.'

'Come on. Let's talk to him,' said Kath, pulling me closer to the
edge of the crowd.

We hovered around in the cold outside the town hall waiting for
the mayor to finish his cycle-race duties. Eventually he moved into
the clear and Kath, braver than I, swooped. I couldn't hear all she
said but it was along the lines that we were New Zealanders called
Bolton, that we lived in The Little Boltons in London, that we had
especially come to Bolton for the weekend, and please could we
have a photo with the Lord Mayor of Bolton.

He looked surprised, interested, even flattered.

'Of course, luv,' he said, gathering in his wife, who had been
standing anonymously nearby, and gesturing to his chauffeur to
take the photo.

What they thought of us — complete strangers with funny
accents — barging up to them like that, I couldn't tell. But
whatever they thought, they acted with friendship and hospitality.
They wanted to take us up to the parlour — what I supposed we
would call the mayoral chambers — but apologised because they
had another appointment and were running out of time. So we
stood chatting in the cold for a few minutes more.

'You elect mayor direct like don't you,' he said to me,
knowledgeably.

'Yes,' I said.

'Not so here you know. Aldermen take turn about. My turn
that's all.'

It may have been just 'his turn' to be mayor but the office
seemed to suit him. He carried out his duties with dignity and
courtesy and represented the interests of Bolton, at least to us, with
the sort of relaxed approach that would make the citizens of any
borough proud.

On our return to The Little Boltons we impressed Mrs Beaumont with our photograph. There, complete with gold chain, was The Lord Mayor of Bolton. There, beside him, was his wife, dressed in an elegant black hounds-tooth cape with her own mini-chain. And there were we, looking cold and plainly dressed, Kath with a plastic Bolton souvenir shopping bag in one hand.

'The Boltons of The Little Boltons in Bolton,' said Kath to Mrs Beaumont. 'With the Lord Mayor of Bolton and his lady wife.'

'They're a handsome couple aren't they, dear,' she said to Kath as she inspected our little photograph.

Kath thought she sounded a little envious, a little proud and a little puzzled. Never before had she known below-stairs staff who knew so many above-stairs type people.

Chapter XXVIII

WE HAD BEEN WARNED ABOUT MRS BEAUMONT'S disability — that she needed the support of a walking frame just to get around the house — and her slight deafness, but we soon discovered that she was otherwise in good general health, not at all frail, and that she was mentally as sharp as a new pin. While we were there her health remained steady and, perhaps because she enjoyed Kath's company and help so much, and was able to get out of the house on a daily ramble, she even seemed to become more positive in her attitude and outlook.

And while we had been warned about Mr Beaumont's irascibility we had not been told — perhaps because nobody knew — about the frailty of his intellectual facilities. At our first meeting, in the living room upstairs, I found him to be, yes, irascible and somewhat absent-minded, but no more than you might expect in a man of his age. Indeed, he said and did some things that were in fact mildly amusing. But it was no laughing matter to watch him slowly get worse even over the few months we were there in his house.

The Beaumonts' doctor was a tall, elegant young woman who looked more like a Vogue model than a physician. She called regularly, sweeping into the house as though it were hers. And although, like most people, she liked and deeply respected Mrs Beaumont, speaking to her as intelligently as the old lady deserved, she positively ordered Mr Beaumont into line with the voice of a primary school teacher. At last I understood why he persisted with his carrot and grapefruit regime: doctor's orders.

She had a double-barrelled name, and fees to match I'm sure, but she was smart and sharp, missing nothing about her patients' symptoms and behaviour. She carried each of their medical histories in her head, quoting dates, symptoms and prescriptions at will. Mrs Beaumont had absolute faith in her — and I could see why — and if patient management and bedside manner were worth money then this young doctor deserved to be a millionaire.

Although we met her many times, the first time we really needed her — in an emergency — she wasn't available. It happened one afternoon when Kath found Mrs Beaumont lying helplessly beside her bed.

'I think I had a little turn, dear,' she said bravely. 'I felt dizzy and woke up here on the floor.'

Kath tried to help her get up but couldn't manage it on her own. So I was called. She was weak and limp, unable to help herself at all, so I had to use all my strength to raise her to a sitting position and get her on the bed. She had indeed taken some sort of 'little turn' and was not feeling at all well. Kath called the doctor — we were given the number along with a lot of other instructions in case of emergency — but she wasn't there. Her secretary told Kath that she was at a meeting.

'Hah,' said Kath to me. 'The Cheltenham Gold Cup's on. I bet she's at a *race* meeting.'

The doctor laughingly admitted as much later.

And so a locum was sent and he decided that Mrs Beaumont should go to hospital for observation. As I carried her bag to the ambulance, walking beside the wheeled stretcher upon which she was being carried, I had a strange feeling; a premonition. And, as she reached out and held my warm hand in her cold one, I sensed that she shared my foreboding. She looked frail and frightened and I thought it was wrong that I should be the one holding her hand at this time.

'Do look after poor Harold, Bob,' she said. 'He does need help you know.'

Even then, so frightened and ill, she was thinking more of her husband than of herself. But I doubted her concern was appreciated or even recognised by Mr Beaumont.

Whatever Mrs Beaumont's problem, though, it wasn't serious and she was back home within a couple of days. But the episode was a sort of omen. It reminded us of how old and vulnerable our employers really were and that it was unlikely — Hermione and

Alice had implied it from the beginning — that we would be at The Little Boltons for very long.

Accordingly, predictably even, the end came nearer when Mr Beaumont too became ill. And his episode was much more serious.

It began one morning when, for the first time in anyone's memory, he was not down to breakfast in time. I knew he was awake and up; I had heard his alarm and listened, with the usual amusement, as he went about his morning unlocking rounds. I even heard the bath running. But he didn't come down to breakfast at the usual time and he was still not there when Mrs Beaumont arrived in the dining room on schedule.

'It's odd that Mr Beaumont isn't down on time, dear, isn't it,' she said to Kath as she served breakfast for one. 'Not like him at all.'

'Would you like Bob to check if he's all right?'

'Oh, no, dear. I don't think so. We'll leave it a little while I think.'

Notwithstanding her husband's unusual and mysterious absence, apparently determined that the house routine should not to be disrupted, Mrs Beaumont tucked into her scrambled eggs with the usual enthusiasm. Preoccupied downstairs with the breakfast routine I was only vaguely aware of Mr Beaumont's absence but Kath was worried and had made a quick reconnoitre of the upstairs floors.

'The old bugger's gone missing,' she reported to me. 'I can't find him anywhere.'

'I heard him in the bathroom before.'

'Well the door's shut—' it was always shut whether he was in there or not '—and I didn't want to open it. But I couldn't hear anything. I even tried to look through the keyhole.'

'What about his clothes. They should be laid out in the study.'

'That's right. I'll check.'

She was back in a flash.

'His clothes are still there,' she reported breathlessly, looking a little worried. 'He's either wandering around the streets in that dreadful old dressing gown or he's snuffed it in the bath.'

'I'd better look,' I said.

Trying hard to restore her professional and detached composure, Kath returned to the dining room. Mrs Beaumont had finished breakfast and was moving slowly to the living room to begin the papers. She stopped in her frame, when Kath came in, and turned around.

'I think Bob better see where my husband is now,' she said.

'He's up there now,' Kath replied, trying not to frighten Mrs Beaumont with what she knew, or, rather, didn't know.

'Oh, good, dear. Well, we better keep his breakfast warm. I'm sure he'll want it before long.' And she resumed her slow shuffle across the room.

Meanwhile I had legged it up to the bathroom landing. I paused, listening at the door. Nothing. Taking a deep breath, anticipating the worst, I turned the old wooden handle and pushed the door. Not locked. It opened. A little. I pushed it open more and — doing the unthinkable — I looked into Mr Beaumont's private bathroom. But I didn't know where to look. I'd never been in this room before. It looked all white and shiny and chromey like a hospital bathroom.

But then:

'Bolton!'

A shout. And I saw him. He was lying in the now cold bath, shivering. His head was almost under the water and his feet were up, resting on the side.

'Damn nuisance,' he said. 'Embarrassing show. Don't know what came over me. Can't seem to get out of the bally thing.'

He couldn't get out of the bath.

I was somewhat ashamed. Kath and I had been certain that he went to the bathroom each morning only as a matter of form. We guessed that he ran the taps to make the right watery noises and then waited for a decent time before coming out, no cleaner than he went in. But on this occasion at least — in fact an all-important Thursday, the change-of-underwear day, the going to town day — we were wrong. He was very obviously in the bath. Stuck in the bath. He couldn't get out.

Ignoring for the moment the watery splashes of bloody-red that were running down the white tiles and making the room look more like an abattoir than a bathroom, and the bloodied water, I tried to be cheerful and positive.

'We'll get you out, Mr Beaumont. No worries,' I said bravely.

But I wondered how. He was cold, wet, slippery, bloody, heavy and weak. But I had to try. And then, I knew, I would have to get him warm. And call the doctor. But in fact getting him out was easy. Once I lent him my arm, and gave him dry towels with which to grasp the towel rails for steadiness, he stepped effortlessly out of the deep, old, enamel-less bath. The problem was not that he didn't have the strength to get out — he had plenty of strength — but that somehow, for some reason, his old mind failing, he had actually forgotten *how* to get out. Instead of standing up and stepping out he had been trying to get out by first throwing his feet over the edge of the bath.

I guessed he had been in the water for an hour-and-a-half. No wonder he was cold. And by using the odd, back-to-front and unsuccessful feet-first method of getting out of the bath he had broken the thin skin of his flailing legs, ankles and feet on the steel taps and had splashed blood all over the room.

We stood together for a moment: he, naked, cold and bleeding, gripping my arm, and dripping water over me. Holding tight to me with one hand, and to a towel rail with the other, he gathered his strength for the move to his study. Looking around at me stiffly, he tried a brave smile.

'I shall never forget you for this, Bill,' he said, gravely.

It was the first time he had ever called me by my first name; and he got it wrong.

'Are you ready to walk now? Or do you need to rest?'

'Sit down I think,' he said, looking around.

I put down the lid of the toilet seat and he sat on that while I helped him put on his robe.

'Are you warm enough?'

'Yes, yes. Getting warm now. What a doings, eh.'

So we waited there together. I was anxious to get downstairs and tell Kath what was going on — I knew she would be worried and would be anxious to reassure Mrs Beaumont — and anxious to get Mr Beaumont warm and into bed. And I wanted to get rid of the bloody bath water and rinse down the tiles before Mariana arrived; I knew the sight would horrify her. But he didn't seem to notice the blood, nor have any pain from his wounds. Instead he sat there in a daze, staring vacantly at the opposite wall. I knew then that something was terribly wrong.

I waited patiently for a while. At last I managed to get him standing again and he walked, holding my arm, to the edge of the landing. The bathroom was on a half floor, up one short flight of stairs from his study, and there was no electric chair. We made the first couple of treads down all right but it was not easy for either of us. He was very unsteady. He stopped and looked at me again with the same grim, feeble and slightly embarrassed grin he had given me in the bathroom. It was a look I had never seen before.

'Sit down I think,' he said.

'On the stairs?'

'Yes, dammit!' It was a shout. A command.

I left him there, halfway down the stairs and leaning against the wall, looking for all the world like a huge Christopher Robin, except for the spread-legged display of his private parts, while I fetched a blanket, covered him with it over his robe, and made my way downstairs as calmly as I could.

I could hear Kath in the living room; she and Mrs Beaumont were obviously waiting for me. I explained Mr Beaumont's situation as best I could, omitting to mention either the blood or his inability to remember how to get out of a bath, while poor Mrs Beaumont, looking increasingly concerned, strained to listen to my words and understand their implications.

'So I think I should get him into bed and call the doctor,' I concluded.

'Yes. I think that's sensible,' said Mrs Beaumont, frowning. 'Don't you, dear?' she added, looking up at Kath with large, frightened eyes, relieved that someone had taken charge.

So Kath called the doctor and I did my best to get the patient to bed. But, as usual with Mr Beaumont, nothing was easy. No matter what I did, no matter how encouraging or how firm I was, he would not move off the stairs.

Abandoning my chores in the kitchen I remained upstairs, lurking in the background, just out of sight, to make sure he didn't faint or fall. Mariana arrived in the meantime and it was strange to see her chatting to him as she worked around him while he continued to sit spread-legged on the stairs, huddled in his blanket.

Eventually, after an hour or so, he was ready to move but angrily resisted my attempts to help. Left alone, while I kept a watching brief from my hiding place in the bedroom, he made his way down to his study where he got dressed. As usual. But slowly. And late.

It was lunchtime when he arrived in the living room where he sat for another hour or so before surrendering to the inevitable and going back to bed without eating breakfast or lunch. The doctor called in the afternoon and, as usual, came downstairs to speak to us privately.

'It's not good,' she said. 'He's perfectly well and strong in his body but his mind's going. He's going to get even more difficult. The family and I really need you two to keep an eye on them both and let us know about any changes.'

Chapter XXIX

BEFORE LONG MR BEAUMONT STOPPED GETTING UP early in the morning. He preferred to sleep. His keys and his former routine were now mine: each morning I had to unlock the house, draw all the drapes, fold away the shutters and collect the papers. It was an eerie feeling to follow his footsteps in this way but it was done to make things seem as normal as possible for Mrs Beaumont.

We offered Mr Beaumont breakfast in bed but he wouldn't take it. He almost stopped eating altogether. Eventually, though, in his own time, he would get up and make his way to his study. There he sat at his desk, ill and confused, his head in his hands, for hours. There was nothing we could do but offer him food and ensure that he was warm and comfortable. He rarely dressed or bathed, being entirely unaware of his personal hygiene and appearance.

Most afternoons he was content to come downstairs and sit in the sun in his old robe and slippers, dozing away the day. He stopped feeding the pigeons. He stopped going to town on Thursdays. He deteriorated as we watched and it was a sad time for us all. Sometimes extreme old age has nothing to recommend it.

Mrs Beaumont was stoical and hopeful, insisting that we maintain all meal timetables. She did her best to jolly her husband along, encouraging him to sit at the table with her at supper and eat something. But he had lost interest in food. I did my best to create things that might be interesting, and easy to eat, serving small portions that would not be too daunting, but without success. Indeed he was in danger of starving or becoming dehydrated.

It was a time of constant worry. When he did sit at the table he frequently fell, tipping lighted candles dangerously across the table. Sometimes he fell to the floor taking his wife with him which meant I had to pick up them both, literally. Willing as we were to help in this and other ways, Mr Beaumont would not accept us in any sort of nursing role.

'I'd rather die than take help from people like you,' he said bitterly on one occasion.

In this he was particularly selfish and foolish; neither of them could manage to live in their house without help, and without willing servants prepared to live with them they would be forced to leave their home. I knew that neither of them would want that.

It was now that our value as 'spies' for the family was realised. We were able to provide evidence and information that could come only from 'inside'.

'They need more help now than we can give them,' we told the family and the doctor, with confidence and authority.

They all agreed and began to work together to find a solution. Meanwhile the poor ill-tempered old bloke began to complain constantly of his aches and pains.

'How are you today, Mr Beaumont?' Mariana asked, only rhetorically.

'Mariana,' he said, rubbing his back, his leg, his arm or his head. 'I have this terrible pain here. And look at this dashed bruise. You know I haven't the Dickens of an idea where it came from.'

'But, Mr Beaumont,' Mariana said helpfully. 'You is fall over yesterday and bruise yourself. Is sore of course.'

That, though, made him angry.

'I did not fall,' he said vehemently. 'I never fall.'

His inability to remember his falls, or his denial of them, meant that every day he rediscovered his myriad pains and bruises and was pathetically mystified by their cause all over again. It was sad to watch this horrible advancement of his illness and I felt sorry for Mrs Beaumont who was powerless to do anything but be kind and sympathetic. But it didn't help. His frustration only increased his anger and he began striking out wildly and irrationally at any perceived slight.

He cared nothing now about household routine, not being a part of it anyway, but got angry when family members began to show their concern by calling more often to the house. They had to pick up his financial affairs too which was not easy as he had lost interest and his files were in disarray. The 'names' of Lloyds — Mr and Mrs Beaumont were both names — were coming under enormous financial and legal pressure at that time and the families were concerned about the state of the old pair's finances.

Now I was having to pick up Mr Beaumont from the floor almost every day. His frequent falls led to more painful bruises, and more anger. While trying hard to maintain the house routine for Mrs Beaumont's sake, we both had to keep an ear listening for the thump and crash that was the signal of yet another fall. Yet while he broke chairs, furniture and china with his crashing tumbles, he never broke anything of himself.

'Dammit all,' he said when once I found him on the floor with a splintered dining chair beneath him. 'I just lost control.'

I thought he was meaning to excuse the fall but he was referring to the loss of control of a much more fundamental function. Solving *that* sort of problem was definitely not for us, even if he would allow it, and a nurse — another New Zealander — was employed to help him get through the day. On Kath's advice she wore a semblance of a uniform and had enough authority to ensure that, if nothing else, he bathed regularly and ate a little. She was an attractive, pleasant, practical, hardworking, strong, capable, get-on-and-do-it young woman and we began to see why New Zealanders were so sought after in this sort of work. But apart from the regular bathing and eating, there was little else he would allow her to do so she remained living in the house only in case of a medical emergency.

It was obvious to us all, nurse included, that he could not go on like this for much longer. So at last we were told that the doctor had arranged that the poor old pair should move to a hospital in Notting Hill. More of a hotel — a luxury hotel — than a hospital, it was a place in which they could be together in their own flat and have the twenty-four hour services of a nurse-cum-maid. It must have cost a small fortune but something had to be done and this was it. Mrs Beaumont was reluctant to go but it was clear, even to her, that unless her husband's health returned there was no choice.

And that, we knew, was the end for us. With the house soon to be empty, our employers installed elsewhere for perhaps the rest of their lives, our time at The Little Boltons was almost over.

Kath helped Mrs Beaumont pack and because they were going to their own self-contained flat she was able to take many personal belongings to make it feel more like home. Mr Beaumont, though, showed no interest. By now compliant enough to simply do what and go where he was told, he left the house — his all-important freehold home for the last fifty years — in a taxi without a backward glance.

We were alone in the house. Mariana was on holiday in Portugal and returned the day after Mr and Mrs Beaumont left.

'I am so sad for Mr and Mrs Beaumont,' she said. 'I think he is going to die in that place isn't it.'

'I think so, yes,' I said.

We had agreed to stay on for a full week to ensure that Mrs Beaumont was settled in the hospital. Whether she and the family had forgotten about Mariana I didn't know, but she, Mariana, turned up to the house each morning, keeping to her regular hours, and together we cleaned and tidied the house ready for it to be closed up.

Kath visited Mrs Beaumont at the hospital each day and we both called in on the last day to say good-bye. Mrs Beaumont was clearly making the most of an unhappy situation in a place she didn't like. Mr Beaumont was sitting in an armchair, as he had sat at home, his head resting in one hand. He didn't look up as we entered nor as we left.

We had bought a campervan and had packed it ready to leave on a touring holiday. After saying good-bye to Mrs Beaumont for the last time we returned to The Little Boltons — now empty, dark, cold and quiet — only to pick up the last of our personal belongings.

We had bought fish and chips and we sat defiantly on the house steps eating our cheap meal directly from the paper wrapper. It was the twenty-fourth of July, nineteen-ninety-two, only five months since, so naive and uncertain, we had first climbed those same steps to press the bell and be drawn by Celia into the warmth of the house. Only five months. But they were five months of our lives that we would never forget.

And then we were gone.

Epilogue

IT WAS THREE MONTHS BEFORE WE RETURNED TO London. I phoned the family to see how Mr and Mrs Beaumont were and we learned that Mr Beaumont had died peacefully in the Notting Hill hospital, during the Notting Hill Carnival, only a month after we had left.

Celia was visiting that day and had entered the bedroom to pray. She had only just begun — speaking her prayers quietly and reverently — when he opened his eyes and focused them on her kneeling at his side.

'What the hell are you doing?' he said, kicking out at her from under the covers.

Thus he ended his life as he had lived it, and I was sad for him only because he had been granted so much and had enjoyed it so little.

After her husband died Mrs Beaumont returned to The Little Boltons and a nurse was employed to take care of her. Mariana, too, was re-employed to take care of the house and it was she who opened the door on our last visit. This time we were welcomed to the living room as guests, sharing tea and cakes with Mrs Beaumont as we had on the day of our interview. But now it all seemed so familiar.

The Monster lumbered up from below, as it always had, and was laden with just the same teapot and china although the cakes and biscuits were factory made. And although Mrs Beaumont still needed her frame and wheelchair, and was perhaps a little more deaf, she otherwise hadn't changed and spoke as quietly and kindly to us both as she always had. She listened with smiling interest, her head to one side and straining forward to hear, as Kath told her briefly all that we had done since we had seen her last. And when we left she grasped my hand tightly and we kissed each other on the cheek.

'You know you did cook such splendid meals for us, Bob,' she said. 'And I didn't appreciate it until we went to that awful hospital.'

And then we went downstairs to see Mariana as so many guests had once come down to see us.

'Oh,' she said as we said good-bye at the area door. 'You have been my best friendis in London and now you are going away. I am going to miss you both so much.'

And she cried and sniffed, and tears streamed from her black eyes and down her beautiful brown face, as she stood at the gate and waved good-bye.

As we walked up The Little Boltons for the last time, past South Bolton Gardens and the gate of Bousfield school, and as I said a silent good-bye to dear Mrs Tiggy-winkle, I noticed that Kath had tears in her eyes. I squeezed her hand and she squeezed mine and we both knew that we had so much to be grateful for. We had seen a side of London we had never expected to see. We had met so many decent, honest, kind and interesting people in England, in London, and in and around The Little Boltons; people we would never forget. We had come to know the members of two families better than we ever deserved. And, above all, we had been granted a unique glimpse into the past and into an English way of life that had now disappeared and could never return.

We kept in touch with Hermione for a while and learned that her mother stayed in the house with a nurse, suffering a few little strokes. Then there was an awful burglary at the house — I couldn't help thinking of the burglar alarm but Hermione didn't mention it — when the nurse was beaten and she, Mrs Beaumont, was roughed up and pulled out of bed.

After that she was moved to a nursing home where she died peacefully, surrounded by her family, on the first day of September, nineteen-ninety-four.

— THE END —

Made in the USA
Monee, IL
07 July 2026